CliffsNotes™
Investing in
IRAs

By Don Andries

IN THIS BOOK

- Understand what an IRA is and how it can help you achieve long-term savings goals
- Figure out what you need for retirement and how you can use an IRA to get there
- Choose the right IRA for your particular savings needs
- Reinforce what you learn with CliffsNotes Review
- Find more information on IRAs and retirement investing in CliffNotes Resource Center and online at www.cliffsnotes.com

IDG Books Worldwide, Inc.
An International Data Group Company
Foster City, CA • Chicago, IL • Indianapolis, IN • New York, NY

About the Author

Donald Andries is a marketing communications consultant. He has served consumer financial institutions in the Chicago area and has opened IRA accounts for customers of the banks he has worked with.

Publisher's Acknowledgments

Editorial

Project Editor: Tracy Barr
Acquisitions Editor: Mark Butler
Associate Acquisitions Editor: Karen Hansen
Technical Editor: J. Patrick Gorman

Production

Indexer: York Production Services, Inc.
Proofreader: York Production Services, Inc.
IDG Books Indianapolis Production Department

Table of Contents

INTRODUCTION

It happens the final quarter of every year. Advice columns about year-end tax strategies compete with articles and advertisements for the holidays. Individual Investment Accounts (IRAs) are always among the options presented for giving a gift to yourself. Why? Because IRAs have proven themselves to be excellent tax-deferred wealth-builders for long-range financial goals such as a first home, a child's education, and a comfortable retirement.

With IRAs, you can benefit from special tax advantages while accumulating earnings for retirement or other long-range financial goals. Unlike regular savings accounts and investments, when you have an IRA, you have to follow certain rules in exchange for the special tax-deferred or tax-free privileges that IRAs offer. This book gives you the information you need to understand IRAs and how having one (or more) can give you tax savings now and help you achieve financial security during retirement.

Why Do You Need This Book?

Can you answer yes to any of these questions?

- Do you want to enjoy financial independence during retirement?

- Do you need to learn about investing in IRAs fast?

- Do you not have time to read 500 pages on long-term investing?

■ Do you want to find out what IRAs are and how they can help you gain financial security?

■ Do you need help understanding the rules that apply to IRAs?

If so, then CliffsNotes Investing in IRAs is for you!

How to Use This Book

With this book, you're the boss. You can read from cover to cover or just look up the information you want, using the Index, the Table of Contents, or just by flipping through the book. To reinforce your learning, check out the Review and Resource Center sections at the back of the book. Also, to find important information quickly, look for these icons in the text:

When you see this icon, make a mental note of this text — it's worth keeping in mind.

This icon alerts you to helpful hints, uncovered secrets, or just good advice.

This icon alerts you to something that you should avoid or that requires special caution.

Don't Miss Our Web Site

Keep up with the ever-changing world of financial planning by visiting the CliffsNotes Web site at www.cliffs-notes.com. Here's what you find:

- Interactive tools that are fun and informative

- Links to interesting Web sites

- Additional resources to help you continue your learning

At www.cliffsnotes.com, you can even register for a new feature called CliffsNotes Daily, which offers you newsletters on a variety of topics, delivered right to your e-mail inbox each business day.

If you haven't yet discovered the Internet and are wondering how to get online, pick up *Getting On the Internet*, new from CliffsNotes. You'll learn just what you need to make your online connection quickly and easily. See you at www.cliffsnotes.com!

CHAPTER 1

UNDERSTANDING IRAS

IN THIS CHAPTER

- ■ Finding out what an IRA is
- ■ Understanding how an IRA works
- ■ Discovering you how can benefit from having an IRA
- ■ Understanding the types of IRAs
- ■ Knowing the differences between an IRA and other retirement plans

IRAs offer special tax-advantaged investment opportunities. The federal government created IRAs to encourage people to save more for retirement and other financial goals. Because of their name — Individual *Retirement* Accounts — many people think of IRAs solely as a vehicle for building retirement income. But investing in IRAs can help you achieve a number of significant financial goals in addition to saving for retirement. By investing in different types of IRAs, you can accumulate money for buying your first home, paying for a college education, and more.

Which IRA is right for you depends on what your financial goals are (save for retirement, buy your first home, or build a college fund). This chapter explains the basic facts about IRAs: what they are, how they work, and why you probably need one.

What an IRA Is

An IRA is a voluntary, tax-advantaged way of saving money for long-term goals. Think of IRAs as investment engines that can accelerate the growth of the money you contribute, helping you realize long-term goals like securing a comfortable retirement, buying your first home, and paying for a college education.

IRAs offer the following advantages:

■ Unlike regular savings, which are taxed in the year of investment and in which growth is taxed annually, IRAs let you enjoy the benefits of tax-free, compounded, long-term growth of funds directed to a variety of investment opportunities.

■ With IRAs, you can lessen your tax burden when you put money in or when you take it out — depending upon what type of IRA (Traditional, Roth, or Education) or what combinations of IRAs you choose.

Although different rules apply to different IRAs, what they all have in common is that you can have any or all of them. And they all provide tax-free growth of earnings. You don't pay yearly taxes on the account balances.

Getting started on IRA investing is easy. Once you do, keeping up the momentum gets even easier as you watch your IRA assets grow.

How an IRA Works

An IRA can begin working for you just as soon as you decide to open one at your bank, at your credit union, or with an investment broker. Essentially, starting an IRA is as simple as going to a savings institution, for example, opening an account, and making your first deposit, or *contribution*. (Chapter 4 has more information about the procedure and paperwork you'll encounter when you open an IRA.)

After you make your first contribution (deposit), the engine starts and accelerates just as fast as you add fuel (that is, more contributions) to it over the years. For example, investing up to $2,000 annually in an IRA can result in fantastic investment growth by the time you reach 65, depending upon when you start your IRA and how wisely you manage your savings and investments.

Obviously, the younger you start, the greater the yield you get. Also, because of compounding, earnings over the life of an IRA can be very good, even if you stop contributing after a number of years (see Table 1-1 for an illustration).

Table 1-1:   How Two IRA Investors Compare

Investor	A	B
Age when starting IRA	26	19
Number of annual contributions @ $2,000 each	40	7 (stops at age 25)
Rate of annual earnings	10%	10%
Assets in IRA by age 65	$894,000	$931,000

The sooner you start retirement savings, the more you'll have at retirement.

What's an IRA worth at age 65 when you start at different ages? Table 1-2 shows you what $2,000 invested annually can grow to if it compounds annually at 8 percent and at 10 percent.

Table 1-2:   IRAs Started at Different Ages

Age IRA Started	Value at 65 Earning 8% Annually	Value at 65 Earning 10% Annually
25	$559,560	$973,702
35	$244,690	$361,886
45	$98,844	$126,004
55	$31,290	$35,052

Obviously, the earlier you start your IRA and the more you contribute over the years, the more you have at retirement. As for how old you have to be to start an IRA, anyone with earned income can do so.

Types of IRAs

IRAs have recently grown into a family of investment products for retirement and other savings goals. Different kinds of IRAs have their own rules for deductible and non-deductible contributions, as well as when and how you can make withdrawals (also called *distributions*). Table 1-3 lists and briefly explains each type of IRA.

But not all IRAs are equal. Some have tax-deferred contributions (meaning you don't pay taxes on the money you put into the IRA when you make your contributions); others don't offer tax-deferred contributions, but *do* offer tax-free withdrawal (meaning that you don't have to pay taxes on the money you withdraw, assuming, of course, that you follow the withdrawal rules).

Before you invest in an IRA, make sure you understand the differences so that you can judge which IRA is best for your specific goals. Table 1-3 gives you a quick run-down of the different types of plans. Head to Chapter 4 for more detailed information on the requirements and rules regarding each of these plans.

Table 1-3:   Types of IRAs Compared

Type of IRA	Tax-deferred contribution	Tax-free withdrawal	Penalty for early withdrawal?
Traditional IRA	Yes	No	Yes, except for home purchase & higher education expense

Type of IRA	Tax-deferred contribution	Tax-free withdrawal	Penalty for early withdrawal?
Roth IRA	No	Yes	Not after first 5 years or for first time home purchase or higher education expenses
Education IRA	No	Yes	No, if limited to education expenses

Traditional IRAs

The traditional IRA is the original individual retirement account. The goal of the traditional IRA is to build retirement income. It best serves people who want to make tax-deferred contributions today and who expect to be in a lower tax bracket during retirement. (Paying taxes on this money when you're in a lower tax bracket lets you pay less.)

■ You can make early withdrawals penalty-free from a Traditional IRA for first-time home purchase (up to $10,000) or qualified higher education expenses.

■ You may begin withdrawals after age 59½ without penalty.

■ You *must* begin what is called "minimum required distributions" when you reach 70½. (Chapter 10 explains how to calculate minimum required distributions.)

Roth IRA

The Roth IRA provides the same tax-free growth of earnings as the Traditional IRA. A ROTH IRA differs from a Traditional IRA in the following ways:

■ You must pay up-front taxes on the money you contribute to a ROTH IRA. Therefore, your ROTH contributions are *not* tax-deferred.

■ When you make qualified Roth IRA withdrawals, they are tax-free, provided that these withdrawals occur after the first five years.

■ You can withdraw money from a ROTH IRA earlier than the five year period — without getting penalized — for things like a down payment on a house and other approved expenses.

■ With a Roth IRA, unlike a Traditional IRA, you, as the account owner, do not have to make distributions during your lifetime.

Table 1-4 shows how a Roth IRA compares to a Traditional IRA as a retirement investment.

Table 1-4:   IRAs as Retirement Investments

Type	Traditional IRA	Roth IRA
Amount contributed	$2,000	$2,000
Tax-advantage rebate @ 22.22% rate	$445	None (contribution is taxable)
Compounded growth rate	9%	9%
Number of years	8	8
Pre-tax balance	$3,985	$3,985
Tax due @22.22% rate	$885	None
After tax balance	$3,100*	$3,985

For more information about the different types of IRAs, head to Chapter 4.

Education IRA

The Education IRA isn't really a retirement account; it's more of an education trust. With the Education IRA, you can save for your child's higher education expenses.

■ You can make contributions of up to $500 annually.

■ You pay taxes on the amount you contribute; therefore, an Education IRA contributions are not tax-deferred.

■ The earnings and qualified withdrawals (or *distributions)* are tax-free. In other words, you don't have to pay taxes on the growth of the account or on withdrawals you make for higher education expenses.

Special IRAs

There are special IRA plans for small business owners and their employees:

■ SEP IRA (Simplified Employee Pension)

■ Simple IRA

■ Keogh Plan

These plans are available to the self-employed, whether or not they employ others. To get a SEP IRA, Simple IRA, or Keogh plan, you either have to fall into one of the follow two categories:

■ You must be the owner of a small business

■ You must be an employee of a small business who offers one of these plans.

Because of these limitations, these plans are not among the chosen IRA options for most individual investors. Chapter 4 has more information about who qualifies for these plans and details about contribution and withdrawals.

Tip

If you do fall into either of these categories, you may want to talk with a financial advisor about starting or contributing to one of these plans. These investment vehicles can offer significant savings advantages depending on your — or your business's — situation.

IRAs versus Other Retirement Plans

If you are an employee earning wages or a salary, you are probably already participating in an employer-sponsored retirement plan. Table 1-5 lists and explains a few of the more common retirement plan options.

Table 1-5:   Other Common Retirement Plan Options

Plan	Description
401(k)	Works like an IRA because participating employees can direct their own investment strategy.
	Includes tax deferral on all contributions, matching employer contributions in most cases, and automatic payroll deduction of employee contributions.
403(b) (Tax Sheltered Annuity Plans)	Offered to employees of religious, charitable, and educational organizations, and public school systems.
	Employees may set aside contributions from their salaries through payroll deduction.
	Contributions are federally and state tax exempt.

But just because you're participating in some other retirement plan doesn't mean you can't benefit from having an IRA. Having the best of all worlds should be your goal in saving for retirement. The following sections explain the main differences between IRAs and other retirement plan options.

How IRAs are different from traditional pension plans

Pension plans are among the earliest forms of employer incentives offered to employees. Some pension funds allow employee contributions as well as the contributions made by employers. An employee is always entitled to the amount of money he or she has contributed to a pension fund. However, all decisions about investment of pension funds are made by employer trustees who must conform to requirements of the Employee Retirement Income Security Act. IRAs differ from pension funds in the following ways:

■ **All IRAs are self-directed.** As the account owner, you make decisions about how much to contribute and when. Most employer-sponsored pension plans can't match this feature.

■ **All your IRA contributions and earnings belong 100 percent to you from day one.** In most employer pension plans, employees are guaranteed a percentage of pension funds, according to their length of service (called *vesting*).

■ **You can convert some IRAs to other types of IRAs without losing your accumulated earnings or paying a penalty.** With the exception of 401(k) plans, most employer pension plans are not designed to allow conversions or "customizing."

■ **Some IRAs enable you to make withdrawals before retirement without penalty**. You can withdraw money penalty-free providing that you withdraw the money for an approved reason such as to fund a first-time home purchase or a child's education. Chapter 4 has more information about withdrawals.

■ **Upon retirement, you get to direct how and when distributions (withdrawals) are made to you.** Employer pension plans often set up annuities to take care of distributions to retirees, relying upon the plan administrator to do this.

Social Security and IRAs

Many people think of Social Security as an important source of retirement income. Although it may be an important component of your retirement income, you should not consider that Social Security alone can provide you with a comfortable or financially secure retirement. According to a 1994 report from the Social Security Administration, Social Security represents 42 percent of income for the average retiree. Others estimate this figure much lower — anywhere from 20 to 30 percent of retirement income.

How much you can expect to receive from Social Security when you retire depends on your income throughout your career. The exact calculation of Social Security benefits is complex. You can get an estimate of yours from the Social Security benefits office (visit www.ssa.gov or call 1-800-772-1213). For a broad estimate, head to the next chapter, where you can find out approximately how much you can expect to receive each year from Social Security.

Social Security won't cover what you need for retirement. It's almost a requirement that everyone who wants to retire in comfort will rely partly upon income from investments, like IRAs.

CHAPTER 2

BUDGETING FOR RETIREMENT

IN THIS CHAPTER

- Planning for a comfortable retirement
- Projecting retirement income
- Projecting retirement expenses
- Finding the money to put into an IRA

Before deciding upon investment for retirement, you need to know where you stand financially right now and where you want to be in the future.

Having IRAs can be good for you and those who may someday benefit from your investment. But just jumping in and opening one or more IRAs without a long-term plan can be counterproductive. This chapter helps you figure out what you have, what you need, and how you can get there.

Estimating What You Need for Retirement

Retirement years can extend well into your 80's — or even 90's. And to sustain a comfortable life style, your retirement income needs to be as much as 70 percent of your current annual income. So, for example, if you earn $40,000 a year, you can expect to need around $28,000 a year to maintain your current lifestyle after you retire.

To figure out what how much money you need for retirement, you need to project what your retirement income and expenses will be. The following sections explain how.

Projecting your monthly retirement income

You must first identify the sources and projected values of your retirement income. In doing this exercise, for example, you want to consider how much you can expect from Social Security, how much you can expect from any pension plans you may have, how much you expect to make if you plan to continue to work through retirement, and so on.

With an estimated retirement income, you can make realistic retirement budget calls. To get an idea of what you can expect, fill in the Projected Monthly Retirement Income Worksheet in Table 2-1.

Table 2-1: Projected Monthly Retirement Income Worksheet

Item	Amount
Social Security	$
Earned income (if you plan to work during retirement)	$
Pension and annuities	$
Retirement assets, like IRAs, and employer defined-contribution plans, such as 401(k) and 403(b)	$
Non-retirement assets (stocks, bonds, and cash for example)	$
Other (rental property income, inheritances, alimony, royalties, etc.)	$
Total projected income	**$**

To fill out this worksheet, project out values for lines 1 through 6 to when you expect retirement to begin. Some people will retire before age 65, others after that age, and others still even later. The following tips can help you in projecting these values.

- Refer to Table 2-2 or contact the Social Security Administration (visit www.ssa.gov or call 1-800-772-1213) for an estimate of your monthly benefits. Ask for the form "Request for Earnings and Benefit Estimate Statement."

- If you have earned income while collecting Social Security benefits before age 70, every dollar you earn over defined limits reduces the amount of Social Security benefits you receive.

Remember

  Be mindful of the $32,000 ceiling on what you can earn during the years you receive Social Security benefits. If you exceed that limit, half your benefits will be taxed. Contact the Social Security Administration for more details.

Table 2-2:   Estimated Social Security Benefits

Average Annual Earnings throughout Career	Approximate Annual Benefit	Estimated Monthly Benefit
$10,000-$20,000	$7,000	$584
$20,000-$30,000	$9,000	$750
$30,000-$40,000	$11,000	$917
$40,000-$50,000	$12,500	$1,042
$50,000-$60,000	$13,500	$1,125
$60,000+	$14,500	$1,208

- You can get pension and annuity projected values from their providers.

- To calculate Line 4, use $1,000 as a basis amount and assume yields averaging 8 percent annually and index for inflation at 4 percent annually (see Table 2-3).

You also may want to visit *Financial Engines* at www.financialengines.com, a new retirement calculator on the Web, which applies risk factors to your plan. Other helpful software sources include *Quicken* (1-800-624-8742) and *Managing Your Money* (1-800-288-6322).

■ For stocks and other investments, consult your broker about what you can expect to continue earning based upon past performance of your holdings. **Note:** Take care not to duplicate values of any investments already included as retirement assets (Line 4).

Table 2-3: Projecting Yields and Purchasing Power

Years	Multiplier 8% yield	Projected Worth	Multiplier 4% index inflation	Adjusted purchasing power
10	2.16	$2160	1.48	$1448
15	3.17	$3170	1.80	$1800
20	4.66	$4660	2.19	$2190
25	6.85	$6850	2.67	$2670

Remember that balances of investments for retirement increase every year they are left to accumulate undisturbed. Don't tap into them until you have exhausted other sources of income.

Projecting your expenses

To project you retirement expenses, use the Projected Annual Retirement Expense Worksheet in Table 2-4:

1. Enter and add up all your variable expenses.

2. Enter and add up all your fixed expenses.

3. Add your fixed expenses to your variable expenses to get your total expenses.

Remember

Your retirement budget should exclude certain expenses that you have now but that will be gone by the time you retire. These types of expenses my include the following:

■ Home mortgage payments

■ Educational expenses

■ Career-related expenses, including things like commuting costs, wardrobe expenses, career-related entertainment expenses, and so on

Of course, retirement today doesn't mean moving into the old people's home. If you retire in good health during your mid to late 60's, chances are you'll pursue an active, leisure lifestyle for 10 years or more. After that, you'll probably relax into gardening and reading. This kind of retirement living will incur some new expenses:

■ Increased travel expenses to visit family

■ Increased leisure expenses for recreation, like golf and tennis

■ Increased property maintenance expenses as the "do-it-yourself" option decreases with age and ability

■ Possible increased medical expenses, over and above what Medicare and Medicaid cover

Table 2-4: Projected Annual Retirement Expense Worksheet

Fixed Expenses	*Projected Amounts*
Mortgage or rent, including property taxes, maintenance assessments, etc.	$
Credit card and installment purchases	$
Insurance, including auto, life, health & accident, homeowners	$

(continued)

Table 2-4: Projected Annual Retirement Expense Worksheet (continued)

Fixed Expenses	Projected Amounts
Savings & Investments	$
Subtotal, Fixed Expenses	$
Variable Expenses	
Food	$
Utilities	$
Home maintenance & improvement	$
Automobile & public transportation	$
Clothing, including purchases, dry cleaning, laundering, etc.	$
Personal care, including hair care & beauty, health club memberships, etc.	$
Medical & dental bills not covered by insurance	$
Entertainment, recreation, and travel	$
Gifts and Contributions	$
Miscellaneous, including pocket money	$
Subtotal, Variable Expenses	$
Total Projected Expenses	**$**

To determine how close you are to meeting your financial goals for retirement, subtract your total projected expenses (from Table 2-4) from your total projected income (from Table 2-1). This gives you a pretty good idea where you stand regarding retirement funds.

Figuring How Much Money You Can Invest Now

This section explains how you can determine where you are now in terms of your ability to begin saving for retirement. In the event that you aren't where you want to be — that is, you don't have money left over for saving — this section also gives you tips on how you can cut back in order to invest in an IRA.

Complete the worksheet shown in Table 2-5. This worksheet gives you a very general idea of where you stand overall right now. Hopefully, you'll discover that you're in a good position to begin investing in an IRA, If that's the case, you can head to the later chapters for information on setting up an account and creating an investment plan. If, on the other hand, you discover that you don't have the money to invest right now — or you want to know how you can scrape together more money for investing — read the following sections.

Table 2-5:   How Much You Can Invest Now

Item	Amount
A. Total Fixed Expenses (Food, shelter, any loan repayments, transportation including car payments, all insurance premiums.)	$
B. Total Discretionary Expenses (Vacation fund, entertainment & dining out, books, clothing, health club, etc.)	$
Total Monthly Expenses	$
Total Monthly Income	$
C. Balance (subtract your expenses from your income) (Add this amount to your savings!)	$

When you do this exercise, be sure to include the things you *must* pay for (**A**), and the things you *dream* about (**B**). Your goal is to get to (**C**), with enough left over to invest in an IRA.

Remember

When you can produce a regular balance after expenses, you are on your way to saving for both short- and long-term goals.

If you discover that you don't currently have enough left over to invest, you need to take a closer look at your finances: Track your income and your expenses. By doing so, you'll have a much better idea where your money is going and where you can cut back.

Track your income

Keep track of what money you have coming in (see Table 2-6). Records of what you receive and its value include check stubs from paychecks, W-2 and tax forms, bank statements, and brokerage statements. Be sure to include any income that you receive, such as alimony, child support, gambling winnings, and so on. This information can help you to separate business from non-business income.

Table 2-6:   Current Monthly Income

Source of Income	Average Monthly Value
Salary or wages after taxes	$
Interest on your checking, savings, and money market accounts	$
Approximate return on investments, such as bonds or mutual funds.	$
Alimony or child support	$
Other	$
Total Monthly Income	$

Track your expenses

Know where your money goes. For starters, take a week (Sunday through Saturday) and keep a detailed record of how you spend your money. If you buy a soft drink or a coffee, write it down. If you take the kids out to a movie, write it down. Every time you hand money over to anybody for any reason, write it down and save all your receipts, for all purchases (including ones you pay for with check and credit cards). When you hit the ATM, write that down, too. At the end of the week, you'll have a pretty good idea where your money goes.

To find out where you can cut back, go back over that weekly outgo and figure out ways to cut back. Maybe buying small soft drinks instead of large or the sale-priced meat instead of the gourmet cut can save, say, $10 a week. Although that $10 a week doesn't sound like much, it can add up to over $500 a year. That's $500 more for saving.

Also examine your monthly spending habits. How much credit card debt do you have? How much to you pay on outstanding loans? What are your monthly bills? Write down everything that you spend (see Table 2-7).

Table 2-7:   Current Monthly Expenses

Expense	Average Monthly Amount
Mortgage or rent and other home expenses	$
Insurance	$
Utilities	$
Groceries and household goods	$
Clothing and personal expenses	$
Entertainment (including dining out) and travel	$
Interest on loans and credit cards	$
Auto expenses (gas, repair, etc.)	$
Childcare	$

(continued)

Table 2-7: Current Monthly Expenses (continued)

Expense	Average Monthly Amount
Other	
1.	$
2.	$
3.	$
Total Expenses	$

Remember

A budget is your key to controlling current and future spending and keeping it in line with your financial goals.

Figure in your assets

Keep track of non-cash assets (see Table 2-8). Know the value of any real estate and/or personal property you own — things like stocks or bonds you have, the value of your home or cars, and so on.

Table 2-8: Non-cash Assets

Types of Asset	Value
Investments (stocks and bonds, mutual funds, and so on	$
Tangible assets (your home, for example), automobiles, boats, jewelry, antiques, home furnishings, etc.	$
Your business or your share in a partnership	$
Deferred assets (401(k) plan, annuities, etc.)	$
Total value of all non-cash assets	$

This amount, in addition to your income and minus your total debts, gives you your *net worth* — a measure of where you stand right now. The higher your net worth, the more likely it is that you will be inspired to budget money for retirement investment.

Getting More Money to Invest

Unless you have a lot of disposable income (and most people don't), you may think that squeezing out additional money to invest in an IRA is nearly impossible. Actually, it's easier than you think. When you know how much money you have coming in and where it's going, you can make decisions that can help you set enough aside to start — and maintain — an IRA. Following are a few suggestions that may be able to help you gather the money you need to begin an IRA:

■ **Cut back or eliminate your credit card debt.** If your interest payments on all short-term credit purchases total $167 a month, you're paying out the same amount you could save for a year to invest in a regular IRA ($2,000).

■ **Give priority to paying off the loan or credit card with the highest interest rate first.** Make the minimum repayments on all the others. When the highest interest debt is paid off, move down the ladder to the next highest. At some point, you might choose to transfer higher interest balances to a single, lower interest rate credit card.

■ **Reduce your short-term debt.** A good short-term savings goal is to reduce your short-term debt for things like cars, boats, furniture, and major appliances. When you pay the items off, continue to pay that amount to yourself.

- **Redirect your money after you've fulfilled your other financial obligations.** For example, as your children finish school, save and invest the money you have been spending on them.

- **Cut back where you can on discretionary expenses, things like entertainment and dining out.** But remember, a budget that leaves no money for an occasional dinner at a nice restaurant or for family outing at an amusement park is destined for failure.

Remember

In building financial security, first make sure that you create a foundation to protect your important assets. This foundation includes an emergency fund and health, life, and disability insurance coverage. Many financial advisors recommend having enough to take care of two month worth of expenses.

Having these resources to fall back on can lessen (if not eliminate) the temptation to "raid" an IRA when times get tough. You can read almost daily about people who take money out of retirement plans prematurely and suffer the consequences of heavy tax penalties.

CHAPTER 3

INVESTIGATING IRAS

IN THIS CHAPTER

- Getting reliable information about IRAs
- Stating your goals
- Deciding who manages your IRA
- Picking a custodian or agent

Before you open an IRA account, you need to get some financial planning advice. Such advice can help you determine how to best proceed to meet your goals. In this chapter, you can find information on where you go for reliable IRA information, what you need to know about yourself *before* you talk with a consultant, and the types of institutions that can manage your IRA investment.

Talking with a Consultant

Fortunately, many sources are available for you when you're ready to sit down and plan your retirement. Bankers, lawyers, securities brokers, insurance agents, CPAs, and other advisors can give sound advice. For the computer savvy, some quality software programs, such as the following,

- Financial Engines (at www.financialengines.com)
- Quicken (at 1-800-624-8742)
- Managing Your Money (at 1-800-288-6322) are also available:

IRA sponsors

Institutions, acting as trustees/custodians, manage IRA accounts for the owners who invest money in these accounts.

■ A trustee/custodian relationship is a legal relationship that exists between banker and depositor, securities broker and investor, and so on.

■ In the case of IRAs, these trustees and custodians are also sometimes referred to as *sponsors* or *agents,* who act on behalf of those — like you — who entrust them with the protection of their accounts.

Any of these IRA sponsor/agents are capable of giving good professional advice. You can also get information on IRAs from any Certified Public Accountant (CPA), whether independent or associated with a financial institution.

Those who sell IRAs have a point of view to sell as well. Balance the advice they give with objective advice you can get on your own, mostly for free, as explained in the following section.

Other sponsors

In addition to getting advice about IRAs from the obvious professionals in the business of selling and managing IRAs, several other sources of information are available, most notably the IRS and your public library. All IRS services are free. Most public library services, except for the cost of photocopies and faxes, are also free.

■ The Internal Revenue Service publishes a variety of publications, forms, and instructions that explain setting up and properly managing retirement programs, including IRAs.
You can contact the IRS through its Web site (www.irs.ustreas.gov) or call 1-800-829-1040 toll free.

- At the IRS Web site, you can select forms and publications for downloading. You can also search publications by topic or keyword.

- At the public library, use the card catalog or ask the reference librarian to help you find books on the subjects of budgeting, savings, and retirement investing for individuals and families.

- If the library has a separate business collection, you can probably find information about retirement planning for the self-employed and small business entrepreneurs.

- In metropolitan areas, most libraries are networked and offer access to the Internet for general and specialized periodicals. Use this service to quickly access full texts of current articles on IRAs and related topics.

You can profit from consulting these resources. In particular, if you intend to pursue "self direction" (in which you, with the help of a professional, direct your own IRA) for maximum investment return, include these sources in you research. See the section "Deciding Who Manages the IRA" for information on self-directed IRAs.

Stating Your Objectives

Before you talk with a consultant, you might want to write down key points about your objectives. Putting your objectives and goals on paper can help you and your advisors identify your best options for IRA investing. Fill out the Objectives Worksheet in Table 3-1 and take this information with you when you talk with a consultant.

Bringing this kind of information can help you and your advisors make the right decisions.

Table 3-1: Objectives Worksheet

Item	Value
Age	
Marital Status	
No./Age Dependents	
Annual Income (before taxes)	
Spouse's income (if you file a joint return)	
Spouse's retirement plans and total current assets (if you file joint return)	
Value of fixed and liquid assets (real estate, personal property, bank account balances, life insurance, etc.)	
Balances of current debt (mortgages, credit card balances, vehicle loans, and other installment loans)	
If you don't own real estate, list your housing expenses	
Employer retirement plans you participate in and total current assets (if you're employed by someone else)	
Any retirement savings plans you have and total current assets (if you're self-employed)	
Your investment knowledge and experience	
Your ability to tolerate risk	
Your interest in managing your assets	
Check the applicable IRA objectives you have	__Build retirement savings __Invest for future home purchase __Save college money for your children or grandchildren

Deciding Who Manages the IRA

More than $1,300 billion in IRA investments are on the books throughout America. By law, IRAs can only be opened and managed with a custodian/agent for the account. In other words, to open an IRA, you must do so through an agent. Who you choose to be your agent depends on a number of factors, such as how involved you want to be in the management of your fund, what type of investments you're interested in, how much risk you're comfortable taking on, and so on. Figure 3-1 shows approximately how current IRA holdings are distributed among the various custodians and agents.

Figure 3-1: IRA custodians and agents.

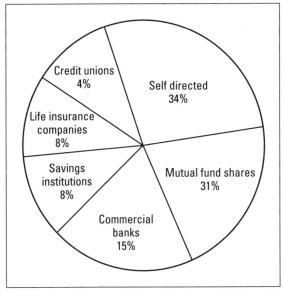

As you can see, most people manage their own IRAs (self-directed) or use mutual fund investment companies as their custodian; the fewest use credit unions for their IRAs. The following sections explain each type of agent.

Self-directed IRAs

With a self-directed IRA, you, as the owner, team up with a cutodian/agent such as a bank, a securities firm, a broker, a CPA, or a financial planner. These professionals help you make sound, profitable investments. If you're interested in a self-directed IRA, keep the following points in mind:

■ As a self-directed IRA owner, you call the shots, choosing what to buy, what to sell, and when.

■ You can invest a self-directed IRA in any type of allowed IRA investment, from long-term, high yield CDs, to stocks and bonds, mutual funds, or even real estate investment trusts.

■ Self-directed IRAs often move from one fiduciary to another — from a bank to a securities firm, for example — as accumulated balances grow.

Remember

The risk of self-directed IRA investing can be high or low, depending upon the choices you make and your custodian/agent's expertise.

Mutual fund shares

Mutual fund investment companies specialize in making a variety of investments in stocks and bonds, and in money-market investments, such as U.S. Treasury bills and bank certificates of deposit (CDs). If you're interested in having one of these companies as your custodian/agent, keep the following points in mind:

■ Mutual fund managers decide how the money is invested and try to provide their shareholders (you) with the highest possible return.

■ Their strategy is to target investments that have varying risk levels and combine them in funds with shares for sale. Yields vary according to fund performance.

Investing in a mutual fund is considered to be safer than investing in individual stocks and bonds but not as safe as investing in a bank, savings association, or credit union.

Commercial banks

Commercial banks are the starting point for many IRA account holders. If you have one or more accounts at a bank, opening an IRA there and getting started is fairly easy. If you're interested in opening an IRA at your bank, keep the following points in mind:

- Most banks offer similar types of long-term IRA investments in CDs, although rates and yields can vary from bank to bank.

- Larger banking concerns offer brokerage services through their own affiliates.

  If this interests you, you may want to investigate whether the bank you're considering offers this service.

- As your IRA account balance grows, the bank can invest some amounts in securities, without moving the account to another custodian/agent (called a *transfer*; see Chapter 7 for information about transfers and rollovers).

The major benefit of having your IRA at a commercial bank is that the federal government insures deposits up to $100,000 for each depositor, providing that the bank belongs to the Federal Reserve System. To find out whether your bank does (many do), look for the FDIC emblem. However, keep in mind that brokerage investments that you make through a bank are *not* insured.

Savings institutions

Savings institutions and savings banks, by law, can offer interest rates on savings deposits that are higher than those that commercial banks offer. The higher interest rate could be an incentive for choosing one of these institutions as your custodian/agent.

Like many commercial banks, savings institutions have their deposits insured by the federal government up to $100,000 for each depositor. Look for the FSLIC emblem.

Life insurance companies

Life insurance companies sell fixed rate and variable rate retirement annuities as IRA investments. With an annuity, the insurance company provides you (and possibly a joint beneficiary) an income for life. Although many types of annuities are available, you are typically guaranteed fixed income payments either for as long as you live or for a fixed period of time. If you're interested in setting up such a plan with an insurance company, keep the following in mind:

■ If you plan to retire early, say at 52, an annuity that pays out equal installments over your lifetime is *not* subject to the 10 percent early tax penalty that would otherwise apply to IRA distributions before age 59½.

■ The risk with this option is about the same as it is for mutual funds shares. How well you do depends upon how well the insurance company does with its investments.

■ If you die early, your beneficiary may or may not receive remaining principal, depending on the type of annuity you have.

Credit Unions

A credit union is a cooperative association that uses funds deposited by its members (who are its sole borrowers or beneficiaries) to make low rate loans to them. Membership is ordinarily restricted to those who meet certain residential or occupational criteria. Like savings banks and savings associations, credit unions can pay higher interest rates on deposits.

Credit union deposits are insured up to $100,000 for each depositor, either by the NCUA (National Credit Union Administration) or a similar insuring agency in the state where the credit union operates.

Choosing a Custodian/Sponsor

Even though we're in the computer age and some people trade in securities from their PC's or Mac's, dealing person-to-person and face-to-face is still a good idea when you are choosing a custodian for something as important as your retirement investing. Visit the local bank, savings institution, or credit union where you already do business and take your list of objectives with you. During your visit, make sure you do the following:

■ Find out what the institution will do for you as a trustee for your IRA.

■ Get the institution's latest rate sheet for savings accounts and CDs.

■ Take notes and bring home the information your banker provides.

■ Review the information and, if you're married, share it with your spouse.

Go to other financial institutions and compare. In your comparison shopping, take special note of the yields offered and methods of interest compounding. One bank may be compounding interest quarterly while another down the street offers the best deal with daily compounding.

CHAPTER 4

STARTING AN IRA

IN THIS CHAPTER

- Understanding the features each type of IRAs offers
- Learning the basics about IRAs for small businesses
- Opening an account
- Keeping necessary records

After you identify your IRA objectives and get advice from IRA professionals and other reliable sources (refer to Chapter 3), you still have to decide which IRA is best for you. This chapter explains the features that each IRA plan offers, It also tells you what to expect when you go to start an account and what bookkeeping chores you need to do. Head to Chapter 5 for suggestions on IRA investment strategies.

Choosing an IRA

You can set up and make contributions to any kind or combination of IRAs if you (or your spouse, if you file a joint return) received taxable wages, salaries, tips, professional fees, bonuses, commissions; taxable alimony, and separate maintenance payments during the year. But with the many choices now available, you need to understand what features each IRA offers.

Traditional IRA

Usually, Traditional IRAs are most attractive to investors who expect to be in a lower tax bracket when they retire. Also, new rules provide for expanded eligibility for spouses and early withdrawals free of IRS penalties for approved expenses, such as a first-time home purchase, higher education costs, or medical disability. Table 4-1 lists the features of a Traditional IRA.

Table 4–1:   Traditional IRA Features

Feature	Description
Eligibility	Anyone under age 70½ with any amount of earned income
Deductibility	Contributions fully deductible if * You're not covered by an employer's retirement plan * If you have a plan at work and are a single filer with income of $31,000 or less * If you have a plan at work and are a joint filer with income of $51,000 or less You can also make non-deductible contributions.
Spouse's contribution	Contribution fully deductible, providing that the following are true: * Your spouse works but *isn't* covered by a plan at work * Your spouse participates in an employer plan, but total combined income is $150,000 or less
Contribution limits	$2,000 per individual annually
Earnings	Tax-deferred until withdrawn Taxed as ordinary income during year withdrawn
Withdrawals allowed	After age 59½ and at death (to beneficiaries) Also for serious disability, qualified first home purchase, or higher education expense

(continued)

Table 4-1: Traditional IRA Features (continued)

Feature	Description
	Otherwise, 10% penalty charged on top of ordinary income taxes for amount withdrawn
Withdrawals required	At age 70½, you must withdraw the lump sum or be making minimum periodic withdrawals; otherwise, you may have to pay 50% excise tax on amount not withdrawn.

Tip

The IRS provides a worksheet for IRA owners to figure deductible and non-deductible contributions to a Traditional IRA. Contact the IRS for a copy of this worksheet (www.irs.gov). Chapter 9 also has a worksheet that can help you keep track of your deductible and non-deductible contributions.

Roth IRA

The Roth IRA may be attractive to you if

- You expect your tax bracket to be the same or higher in retirement.

- You expect not to use IRA withdrawals in the near future.

- You want to leave the IRA to your heirs.

Table 4-2 lists the features of a Roth IRA.

Table 4-2: Roth IRA Features

Feature	Description
Eligibility	No age restriction.
	Anyone with earned income, with the following limits:

Feature	Description
	$150,000 or less for joint filers
	$95,000 or less for single filers
	$10,000 or less for spouses filing separately
Deductibility	Contributions are not tax deductible.
Spouse's Contribution	Contributions are not tax deductible.
Contribution Limits	$2,000 per individual annually. **Note:** Amount reduced by any contribution made the same year to a Traditional IRA.
Earnings	Earnings grow tax free. *Qualified* withdrawals are also tax-free.
Withdrawals	The following withdrawals (distributions) are tax free: * Those made *after* the 5-taxable-year period * Those beginning at age 59½ * Those made because of disability or after your death * Those made toward first-time home purchase for you or a family member (limited to $10,000 and home must be primary residence)
Required withdrawals	There are no required minimum distribution rules for withdrawals from a Roth IRA during the account owner's lifetime.

Remember

With the Roth IRA, you are not be required to pay income taxes on the growth of the account, provided you follow the rules for qualified withdrawals.

Tip

A non-deductible IRA may be a good additional choice for those covered by a pension or other employer plan and who want to accumulate tax-deferred earnings for a more comfortable retirement.

Education IRA

An Education IRA is not a retirement arrangement. It is a trust or custodial account created for paying higher education expenses of a designated beneficiary. You can set up Education IRAs for as many beneficiaries as you like. Table 4-3 lists the features of an Education IRA.

Table 4-3:   Education IRA Features

Feature	Description
Eligibility	Any individual on behalf of a child under 18.
	Contribution to qualified state tuition program not allowed in same year.
	Income limit phase outs at $95,000 to $110,000 for single filers; $150,00 to $160,000 for joint filers.
Deductibility	Contributions are not deductible.
Contribution limits	$500 per child until child's 18th birthday.
	Not subject to reduction by contributions to any other IRAs.
Earnings	Earnings accumulate tax-free.
Withdrawals allowed	Tax-free withdrawals allowed if used for qualified higher education expenses prior to the child's 30th birthday.

Special IRAs for Small Business

If you are self-employed, you may want to take advantage of IRA accounts designed specifically for small businesses:

- SEP IRA

- SIMPLE IRA

- Keogh Plan

If you are interested in pursuing one of the preceding special plans, consult your employer and/or tax advisor. Because of their special requirements, these plans are more complex for you to manage than a Traditional, Roth, or Education IRA. However, their higher contribution limits are more than worth the effort if you qualify.

SEP IRA

A SEP-IRA has most features of a Traditional IRA except for contribution limits. Table 4-4 lists the basic features of a SEP-IRA.

Table 4-4:   SEP-IRA Features

Feature	Description
Eligibility	Any self-employed individual
Deductibility	Annual contributions fully deductible, within contribution limits
Contribution limits	Up to 15% of your earnings or $30,000, whichever is less
	Can still make annual contributions to other IRAs you have
Special rules	If you hire employees, the employees must be allowed into the plan
	You pay a penalty if you exceed your maximum allowed contribution.

Tip

If you are a sole proprietor and have no employees, a SEP IRA is the best choice for your retirement investments.

SIMPLE IRA

A SIMPLE IRA is for employers with up to 100 employees who earn at least $5,000 in the preceding calendar year. Table 4-5 lists the basic features of a SIMPLE IRA.

Table 4-5: SIMPLE IRA Features

Feature	Description
Eligibility	Employees receiving $5,000 or more per year may choose to participate.
Deductibility	Pre-tax salary reduction plan. No further deductions from taxable income.
Contribution limits	$6,000 per employee per year, deducted from gross salary before taxes.
Special rules	Generally, employer does either of the following: Matches employee contributions up to 3% of employee's gross annual compensation Makes fixed non-elective contributions equaling 2% of the employee's compensation.

Remember

Avoid making excess contributions to any type of IRA. Excess contributions and their resulting earnings are generally subject to a 6 percent excise tax. To avoid this tax, you must withdraw all the excess by the due date for your tax return of the year when the excess contribution(s) were made.

Keogh Plan

Originally for the self-employed, but now available to corporations, Keogh plans are more complex than SEP-IRA and SIMPLE IRA plans. Table 4-6 lists the main features of a Keogh Plan.

Table 4-6: **Keogh Plan Features**

Feature	Description
Eligibility	Self-employed individual, not incorporated.
Deductibility	Yes, up to contribution limits below.
Contribution limits	Up to $30,000 or 25% of self-employed income, whichever is less.
Special rules	If self-employed person has employees, those who qualify under written plan must be allowed to participate in plan.

If you are interested in setting up or participating in a Keogh plan, be sure to talk to a financial advisor.

Setting Up an Account

Although the specifics of setting up an account may differ slightly depending on what type of IRA you're opening and what institution you're using as the custodian of the account, the basic experience is the same. For example, suppose that the following applies to you:

- You are opening a self-directed Traditional IRA and/or a ROTH IRA.

- Your trustee/custodian is either your local bank or credit union.

The following sections explain what you can expect when you open the account.

You can open an IRA with any minimum deposit allowed by the custodian institution. You don't necessarily have to deposit $2,000 — the maximum yearly contribution for an individual.

The disclosure statement

You get a disclosure statement that describes the general rules and basic tax considerations governing Traditional IRAs and Roth IRAs.

This document is generally quite lengthy. Take the disclosure statement home overnight to digest all the key points.

The application

You have to complete and sign an application to open an IRA account at the bank or credit union. (The custodian's representative must also sign, accepting your account.) This application includes the following:

- The Type of IRA account you're opening

- The amount of your initial contribution

- The designation of beneficiaries (You can name different beneficiaries for each IRA you own, or you can have the same beneficiary for all.)

If you are opening more than one IRA, you have to fill out a separate application for each one.

The Custodial Agreement

You have to sign a Custodial Agreement if it is not included in the application. This agreement establishes the fiduciary relationship between you as the account owner and the custodial institution where your account is managed.

Other forms

If contributions or deposits going to your new account are currently with other custodial institutions, you have to fill out and sign the necessary transfer and rollover forms. These forms allow the institution where you are opening the new IRA (or IRAs) to transfer the funds from your old IRA accounts to the new accounts you are opening. For information about transfers and rollovers, go to Chapter 7.

Basic Bookkeeping Tasks

Keeping good records of your IRA contributions is very important. These records can help you verify the status of each IRA you own. This information is beneficial for the following reasons:

■ If the IRS ever questions you about your IRAs, these records provide ready answers.

■ When the time comes for withdrawals from any of your IRAs, these records help you distinguish between earnings and contributions so that you can pinpoint taxable and non-taxable amounts that are withdrawn.

Be sure to secure these files in a fireproof container or in your bank safety deposit box.

The following sections offer a few other tips for keeping track of your IRA.

Keep beneficiaries up to date

When you start an IRA account, you must name a beneficiary. Whenever you decide to change the beneficiary, notify the fiduciary of your IRA about changes you want, always in writing.

You may want to have a witness (spouse, relative, or trusted friend) also sign this document to avoid any doubt of your intentions.

Establish a record-keeping system

As long as you own an IRA, be sure to keep the following for your own records:

- **A copy of each tax return you file.** You automatically record your contributions on your federal income tax return.

- **All transaction receipts and statements for each IRA you own.** If your trustee unintentionally mislays a required document, your backup record becomes a primary source if the IRS has a question.

CHAPTER 5

GENERAL INVESTMENT GUIDELINES

IN THIS CHAPTER

- Understanding basic investment strategies
- Minimizing your risk and increasing your returns
- Knowing what you can and can't invest in
- Discovering the benefits of having multiple IRAs

IRA investors range from people with little or no knowledge of the financial world to sophisticates who play the stock market via the Internet on their PCs. In this world of targeted marketing, everyone is bombarded with offers of get rich quick investments. Considering all of this and the fact that you can't spend all of your time directing your IRA investments, this chapter contains some basic strategies to follow.

Determining How Much Risk You Can (Or Should) Take

In investing for retirement, people all start at different ages. To maximize your investment, you need to know what stage you're in and how much risk you can afford to take. (See the section "What You Can and Can't Invest In" for an explanation of the types of investments and the level of risk associated with each.)

The young investor (your 20s)

Young investors with no family and no other responsibilities other than earning a wage — and who have many years before retirement — may want to have their IRA contributions in a riskier investment in order to maximize growth.

The middle investor (30s and 40s)

A family that has education fees, mortgage costs, and so on, may want to take a more conservative approach, such as investing in mutual funds. However, they may not want to go too conservative because they still need to take risks to ensure the high to moderate growth that is necessary to fund a child's education or to pay for a healthy retirement.

If you fall into this category, you have a double challenge:

■ You need to protect yourself from excessive risk. At the same time, you need to ensure substantial growth.

This is a time when investing is vitally important, even though you may have other significant financial obligations such as mortgage payments and education costs. If you don't contribute much to your retirement plan during this time, you'll have a hard time catching up in your later years.

Older investors (50s and 60s)

The empty-nester who has sent the kids through college and who must now protect the IRA investment may want to invest more conservatively — that is, in things that have less risk — in order to hold onto all they have built up. If you fall into this category, for example, you may decide to invest in CDs, which are low-risk. (Of course, if you've been able to save effectively throughout your life, and your net worth is large, reducing your investment risk may be less of a concern.)

Basic Strategies for IRA Investing

Once you open an IRA (or IRAs), develop a steady strategy for investing in them. For example, one way to make sure that you contribute what you want (and can) into your IRA is to make monthly deposits. If you plan to invest $1,000 a year, making monthly deposits of $83 dollars is much easier than making an annual deposit of $1,000. Following are a few other general guidelines you can follow to make the most out of your IRA:

■ **Make your IRA contribution early each year.** For example, if you prefer to make one annual deposit rather than incremental deposits, contribute to your IRA in January. Doing so lets you get 12 full months of earning interest and compounding.

■ **Don't stop adding to your IRA after you begin withdrawals or retire.** Keep contributing to Traditional IRAs until 70½, which is when you must stop contributing. Contribute to your Roth IRAs as long as you live, if you want.

■ **Go for high yield investments.** Pick some investments that pay current income, like time deposits, to best utilize IRA tax-free compounding and sheltering of profits.

■ **Diversify.** Choose several types of investments to spread your risk. See the later section "Diversifying your investments" for information on diversifying.

■ **Be alert to changes.** Understand the financial world you live in so that you can make timely choices for your IRA.

■ **Control your assets.** Take some time each week to monitor your IRA investments. Table 5-1 shows an IRA investment log that can help you keep track of your accounts. Keep one of these for each account and for each year you have the account.

- Avoid directing IRA assets to tax sheltered and/or tax-deferred investments. These types of investments include things like municipal bonds, tax-free money funds, and tax-deferred annuities. You gain nothing by putting them in an IRA because they're already tax-free or tax-deferred.

Table 5-1:   IRA Investment Log   Year_____

Financial Institution: _____	Contact Person: _____
Date Opened: _____	Type of Investment: _____
Beneficiary _____	

Account Information

Initial Investment Amount:	$_____
Contributions:	$_____ Date: _____
	$_____ Date: _____
	$_____ Date: _____
	$_____ Date: _____
Fees:	$_____
Withdrawals/Penalties	$_____
Rate of Return (%)	_____
Value Jan. 1:	$_____
Value Dec. 31	$_____

What You Can and Can't Invest In

A broad range of investments is permitted for funds deposited in IRA accounts. Table 5-2 lists some of the more common types of IRA investments. The items in this table are arranged from lower to higher risk.

Table 5-2:   IRA Investment Options

Option	Description	Comments
Regular savings	Simple interest bearing accounts that offer safely and liquidity. You can open a savings account with little as $50. Principal and interest are fully insured.	A great way to start an IRA if you don't have much to invest
CDs	Can be purchased for IRAs with minimums as low as $500. Offer fixed rates of return (yields) over specified time periods (from 30 days to five years maturity). Interest compounded anywhere from daily to quarterly, depending upon the financial institution. Fully insured.	You may face penalties for transferring or withdrawing these funds before the CD's maturity date.

Money market funds	Pay the short-term money market rate, usually slightly below the U.S. Treasury bill rate.	Offers great liquidity.
	Yields are constantly changing with market conditions.	Great when rates are high; when interest rates fall, not so good.
	Can switch funds to another investment without waiting for maturity date.	
	Usually insured.	
Mutual fund shares and stocks	More risk and potentially higher yields are afforded by mutal fund shares and the stock market.	Consult financial advisors before investing in these.
	Uninsured.	

You can also invest in the following:

- Government securities, such as U.S. Treasury bills, notes, and bonds in addition to U.S. government agency bonds

- Securities traded on stock exchanges or over-the-counter market

- Certain types of unit investment trusts

- Annuity contracts meeting U.S. Revenue Code requirements (including insurance annuity contracts)

- Gold and silver coins issued by the U.S. Treasury

Warning

Other investments are not permitted for IRAs. These include the following:

- Life insurance contracts

- Collectibles such as art works, rugs, antiques, metals, gems, stamps, certain coins and bullion

- Alcoholic beverages

- Certain other tangible personal property, such as real estate owned directly by you

Prohibited Transactions

In addition to investments that are off-limits for IRAs (as the preceding section explains), certain transactions are generally prohibited. The following lists the types of transactions that are not permitted or that can result in a significant penalty:

- Borrowing money from an IRA

- Selling property to an IRA

- Using an IRA as security for a loan

- Making excess IRA contributions

- Making early withdrawals (premature distributions)

- Failing to make required withdrawals or withdrawing less than you should

Engaging in a prohibited transaction may result in sudden "death" for a Traditional IRA, turning its assets into ordinary income for that year. The account stops being an IRA as of the first day of the year in which the prohibited transaction was made.

Minimizing Your Risk

You can do a few things to help minimize the risk for your entire IRA portfolio. The following sections tell you how.

Diversify your investments

Similar to not putting all your eggs in one basket, you don't want to put all your IRA assets in one type of investment. If you invest everything in CDs, for example, and rates drop, your IRA assets take a nose dive.

When you spread your IRA assets into several kinds of investments it's called *diversifying*. Diversifying is especially important when your IRA portfolio has grown to a respectable amount. When you diversify, consider dividing your IRA assets into thirds (see Figure 5-1):

- One third in insured Certificates of Deposit, maturing from one to three years

- Another third divided between mutual funds and money market investments

- The final third invested in stocks and bonds

Invest in multiple IRAs

Don't hesitate to have more than one IRA, each having separate custodians. See the section "Investing in More than One IRA" for information.

Invest both for income and for growth

Income investments like insured CDs, money market funds, and government securities make the most efficient use of tax-free compounding as your IRAs grow. When inflation grows, however, these types of investments become less productive.

Growth investments, on the other hand, offer more protection against inflation. Going into mutual funds that invest in stocks and buying stocks yourself are the best options for growth.

Figure 5-1: How to divide your investment.

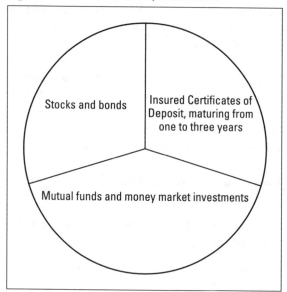

Hedge your bets on interest rates

Whether interest rates will go up or down is anybody's guess. As the experts say, "Keep your eye on the fed (Federal Reserve Board)."

- If you think interest rates will fall, invest in a fixed rate Certificate of Deposit (CD). There's no doubt about its worth when it matures.

- If you think interest rates will rise, buy a variable rate CD. If rates do indeed rise, you'll get an even higher rate as this investment nears the end of its term.

Your best bet would be to put half of an IRA's assets into a fixed-rate and the other half in a variable rate CD. You'll come out better than if you had put all the money on the one that ends up in second place.

Investing as Your IRA's Value Grows

Most custodians renew the CD at current rates if they don't receive instructions from you otherwise within 10 days of maturity. To make sure that you rather than your custodian gets to make this decision, log the maturity date of your CDs in your records and be prepared to renew or move on to something else.

If you are a younger investor and can ride through short-term losses, stocks offer proven long-term growth. If you want to earn an average of 8 to 10 percent on your IRA investments, do some research or get some good advice about stocks that have long, unbroken dividend-paying records.

Investing in More than One IRA

You can own as many IRAs as you like, providing you follow the rules. As a rule, active IRA investors generally have more than one IRA. Once you understand the kinds of IRAs that best suit your investment objectives, you can decide which ones to open and how to allocate contributions to each of them. For example, you may elect to have a Traditional or Roth IRA that you direct for retirement investment. And if you have children, you probably want to add on an Education IRA for each child in the family.

Regardless of the number of IRAs you set up, keep the following in mind:

■ The contribution limit is set by law. If you have more than one IRA, the limit applies to the total contributions to all Traditional and Roth IRAs for the year.

Remember

The limits ($2,000 and $4,000) can be reduced if you or your spouse is covered by a qualified retirement plan at work. You can find worksheets for figuring deductible and non-deductible contribution limits in Chapter 1 of IRS Publication 590, available free. Table 5-3 shows the phase-out schedule for deductible contributions for 1998.

Table 5-3: IRA Deductibility and Eligibility Rules

Adjusted Gross Income (AGI)	Traditional IRA	Roth IRA
0-$30,000	Contributions deductible for everyone	Eligible*
$30,000-$40,000	Contributions deductible for joint filers Deductibility phase-out range for single taxpayers - who participate in employer sponsored pension plans	Eligible*
$40,000 $50,000-	Contributions deductible for joint filers	Eligible*

Adjusted Gross Income (AGI)	Traditional IRA	Roth IRA
$50,000-$60,000	Deductibility phase-out range for joint filers	Eligible*
$60,000-$140,000	Contributions deductible only if taxpayer isn't an active participant in an employer-sponsored pension plan	Eligible*
$150,000-$160,000	Deductibility phase-out range	Eligibility phase-out range
$160,000-$190,000	Contributions deductible only if taxpayer and spouse aren't active participants in an employer-sponsored pension plan	Not eligible

* Single taxpayer eligibility phases out between $95,000-$110,000.

To figure out your maximum contributions for multiple IRAs, you have to calculate your *modified adjusted gross income* (MAGI). See Chapter 7 for instructions.

- You have greater flexibility in managing your investments when you have more than one IRA. However, you also have multiple custodial trustees and custodial fees.

- In addition to owning Traditional, Roth, and Education IRAs, you can own a SIMPLE IRA set up by an employer. If you are self-employed, you can have a SEP IRA.

CHAPTER 6

PAYING TAXES ON IRAS

IN THIS CHAPTER

- Understanding when and how IRAs are taxed
- Getting more information on IRA taxes
- Avoiding penalties
- Knowing what IRS forms to file with your tax return

These IRA features — tax-deductible contributions and tax-free earnings — enable you to gain the maximum return on your IRA investments. But there's no such thing as a free lunch. That goes for IRAs as well. The IRS is the final authority on rules affecting IRAs, especially regarding what is and isn't taxable. This chapter explains what taxes you can expect to pay and when.

Getting Answers from the Feds

Because the IRS really wants to help taxpayers avoid problems, they provide free publications and publish their rulings on questionable IRA transactions as they occur. The IRS has the following free publications available to the serious IRA owner:

- Publication 590, "Individual Retirement Arrangements (IRAs) including Roth IRAs and Education IRAs"
- Publication 560, "Retirement Plans for Small Business (SEP, SIMPLE, and Keogh Plans)"
- Publication 552, "Record Keeping for Individuals"

You can order any of these or other titles by mail. You can also go to the IRS Web site (www.irs.gov) to browse or download them.

When and What Taxes Are Due

Tax-deferred contributions to a Traditional IRA are exactly that — *deferred,* or put off until you start to withdraw dollars from the account. Then you have to pay taxes on the amounts you withdraw in the year or years of withdrawal. However, because *non-deductible* Traditional IRA contributions are taxable when you deposit them in the IRA, they've already paid their way. When you withdraw these funds, you don't have to pay taxes on them.

It's very important that you keep track of deductible and non-deductible IRA contributions so that you pay only the taxes you are required to pay.

When you receive a distribution from any Traditional IRA, you receive Form 1099-R or a similar statement (see Figure 6-1). This form identifies what kind of distribution has been made, what amount is taxable, and any prohibited transactions that were made.

Figure 6-1:   Instructions for using this information appear on Form 1099-R.

☐099 ☐ VOID ☐ CORRECTED			

PAYER'S name, street address, city, state, and ZIP code	1 Gross distribution $	OMB No. 1545-0119	Distributions From Pensions, Annuities, Retirement or Profit-Sharing Plans, IRAs, Insurance Contracts, etc.
	2a Taxable amount $	19**99** Form **1099-R**	
	2b Taxable amount not determined ☐	Total distribution ☐	**Copy A**
PAYER'S Federal identification number	RECIPIENT'S identification number	3 Capital gain (included in box 2a) $	4 Federal income tax withheld $	**For Internal Revenue Service Center**
RECIPIENT'S name		5 Employee contributions or insurance premiums $	6 Net unrealized appreciation in employer's securities $	File with Form 1096. For Privacy Act and Paperwork Reduction Act Notice and instructions for completing this form, see the **1999 Instructions for Forms 1099, 1098, 5498, and W-2G.**
Street address (including apt. no.)		7 Distribution code IRA/ SEP/ SIMPLE ☐	8 Other $ %	
City, state, and ZIP code		9a Your percentage of total distribution %	9b Total employee contributions $	
Account number (optional)		10 State tax withheld $ $	11 State/Payer's state no.	12 State distribution $ $
		13 Local tax withheld $ $	14 Name of locality $	15 Local distribution $

Form **1099-R**   Cat. No. 14436Q   Department of the Treasury - Internal Revenue Service

Do NOT Cut or Separate Forms on This Page — Do NOT Cut or Separate Forms on This Page

Because Roth IRAs and Education IRAs are both limited to non-deductible contributions, they pay their taxes as they go, so to speak. Earnings and withdrawals from these two types of IRAs are generally tax-free if you use them for qualified purposes.

Traditional IRAs and taxes

When you make tax-deferred contributions to your Traditional IRA, you don't pay taxes on the contribution amount. But when you withdraw money from the IRA (called a *distribution*), you must pay taxes.

■ You include traditional IRA distributions in your gross income in the year you receive them.

■ Traditional IRA distributions get no special treatment. You treat them as regular income.

Distributions from your Traditional IRA may be fully or partly taxable depending upon whether your IRA includes any non-deductible contributions:

■ If you made only deductible contributions, your distributions are fully taxable.

■ If you made any non-deductible contributions, the distributions are partly taxable.

■ If you made non-deductible contributions (that is, you paid taxes on the money you contributed), the amounts of these are not taxed when distributed. (In other words, the IRS isn't going to tax you twice.) However, the *earnings* from non-deductible contributions *are* taxed.

■ If you have a loss on your Traditional IRA investment for whatever reason, you can recognize the loss on your income tax return. You can only do this, however, when *all amounts in all your Traditional IRA accounts* have been distributed to you.

To figure the taxable and non-taxable amounts of your distribution in a given year, you must use IRS Form 8606, shown in Figure 6-2, and a helpful "Worksheet to Figure Taxable Part of Distribution" found in Chapter 1 of Publication 590.

Remember

If you inherit an interest in a Traditional IRA from your spouse, you can treat the entire inherited interest as your own IRA. It is then subject to all the regular rules for tax treatment of Traditional IRAs. However, other beneficiaries of Traditional IRAs must include distributions they receive in their gross income for the year in which they receive them.

Figure 6-2: Form 8606.

Form **8606**	**Nondeductible IRAs**	OMB No. 1545-1007
Department of the Treasury Internal Revenue Service (99)	▶ See separate instructions. ▶ Attach to Form 1040, Form 1040A, or Form 1040NR.	19**98** Attachment Sequence No. **48**

Name. If married, file a separate Form 8606 for each spouse who is required to file Form 8606. See page 4 of the instructions. | Your social security number

Fill in Your Address Only if You Are Filing This Form by Itself and Not With Your Tax Return

Home address (number and street, or P.O. box if mail is not delivered to your home) | Apt. no.

City, town or post office, state, and ZIP code

Part I Traditional IRAs (Nondeductible Contributions, Distributions, and Basis)

Caution: *If you converted part or all of your traditional IRAs to Roth IRAs in 1998, see the instructions for Part II on page 5 before making entries in Part I.*

1 Enter your nondeductible contributions to traditional IRAs for 1998, including those made during 1/1/99±4/15/99 that were for 1998. See page 4 ..... | 1 |
2 Enter your total IRA basis for 1997 and earlier years. See page 5 ..... | 2 |
3 Add lines 1 and 2 ..... | 3 |

> Did you receive any distributions (withdrawals) from traditional IRAs in 1998? — No ▶ Enter the amount from line 3 on line 12. Do not complete the rest of Part I.
> — Yes ▶ Go to line 4.

4 Enter only those contributions included on line 1 that were made during 1/1/99±4/15/99. See page 5 | 4 |
5 Subtract line 4 from line 3 ..... | 5 |
6 Enter the total value of **ALL** your traditional IRAs as of 12/31/98 plus any outstanding rollovers. See page 5 ..... | 6 |
7 Enter the total distributions you received from traditional IRAs during 1998. Do not include amounts rolled over. See page 5 ..... | 7 |
8 Add lines 6 and 7 ..... | 8 |
9 Divide line 5 by line 8 and enter the result as a decimal (rounded to at least 3 places). Do not enter more than ™₹.000₹ ..... | 9 | × . |
10 Multiply line 7 by line 9. This is the amount of your nontaxable distributions for 1998 ..... | 10 |
11 Subtract line 10 from line 5. This is the basis in your traditional IRA(s) as of 12/31/98 ..... | 11 |
12 Add lines 4 and 11. This is your **total basis in traditional IRAs for 1998 and earlier years** ..... | 12 |
13 **Taxable amount.** Subtract line 10 from line 7. Enter the result here. Also include it in the total on Form 1040, line 15b; Form 1040A, line 10b; or Form 1040NR, line 16b ..... | 13 |

Part II Conversions from Traditional IRAs to Roth IRAs

Before you begin, see page 5 if: **(1)** your filing status is married filing separately, **(2)** your modified AGI is more than $100,000, **(3)** you converted only part of your traditional IRAs to Roth IRAs, or **(4)** you received any distributions (withdrawals) from traditional IRAs during 1998.

14a Enter the total amount of distributions from traditional IRAs during 1998 that were converted to Roth IRAs ..... | 14a |
b Recharacterizations. See page 3 ..... | 14b |
c Subtract line 14b from line 14a ..... | 14c |
15 Enter your basis in the amount you entered on line 14c. See pages 5 and 6 ..... | 15 |
16 **Taxable amount of conversions.** Subtract line 15 from line 14c ..... | 16 |
17 **Amount subject to tax in 1998.** Check here if you elect **NOT** to spread the taxable amount on line 16 over 4 years (see page 6) ..... ▶ ☐
If you checked the box, enter the amount from line 16 on line 17. Otherwise, enter 25% (0.25) of line 16 on line 17. Include the line 17 amount in the total on Form 1040, line 15b; Form 1040A, line 10b; or Form 1040NR, line 16b ..... | 17 |

For Paperwork Reduction Act Notice, see page 8. | Cat. No. 63966F | Form **8606** (1998)

Roth IRAs and taxes

All Roth IRAs' contributions are non-deductible, meaning taxes are paid when you make your contributions. There are no taxes on the growth of your Roth IRA, and no taxes upon withdrawals (distributions), provided you follow the rules.

Therefore, you do not include the following in your gross income:

■ Qualified distributions (see Chapter 4 for information about what constitutes a qualified distribution)

■ Distributions that are a return of your regular contributions

You may have to pay taxes (and penalties) on this money, however, in the following circumstances:

■ You make withdrawals within the first 5 years of opening the account.

■ You make withdrawals before 59½, except when used for qualified home purchase or higher education expense.

■ You make excess contributions (any that exceed the allowed limit).

You can correct an excess contribution by withdrawing the excess before filing your tax return. Your withdrawal must include any earnings on the excess. If you accomplish this before the due date of your tax return, you don't have to pay the 6 percent excise tax.

As an owner of a Roth IRA, you are not required to take any distributions during your lifetime.

Education IRAs and Taxes

Contributions to Education IRAs are non-deductible, which means you pay taxes on these amounts when you make your contributions. Generally, a withdrawal is tax-free if it doesn't exceed the beneficiary's qualified higher education expenses in a tax year. (The beneficiary of an Education IRA is the person whose education the money is paying for.) If the total withdrawals for a tax year are more than the expenses, a portion of the amount is taxable to the beneficiary.

A 6-percent excise tax is applied each year to excess contributions you make to an Education IRA (the contribution limit is $500 annually). If you discover you've made an excess contribution in any given year, you can correct it the same way you correct excess contributions to ROTH IRA. See the preceding section for details.

Special tax situations

If you buy an annuity contract with your Traditional IRA assets, you are not taxed when you receive the annuity contract. You are taxed when you start receiving payments from the annuity contract. Annuity payments can be partly taxable if you made both deductible and non-deductible contributions to Traditional IRAs. If you made only non-deductible contributions, the annuity payments to you are fully taxable.

Reporting and Withholding for Taxable Amounts

Reporting and withholding rules about taxable events in the life of your IRAs are quite detailed and specific.

You must report fully taxable distributions on your tax return (Form 1040 or 1040A) in addition to filling out and filing Form 8606 and also filing a copy of Form 1099-R, as explained in Table 6-1.

Table 6-1:   Tax Forms You Need to File

Form	Required When
Form 8606	You make any non-deductible contributions to a Traditional IRA
	You convert all or part of assets in a Traditional IRA (or SIMPLE IRA) to a Roth IRA
Form 8606 Form 1099-R	You receive distributions from a Traditional IRA, and you also have made non-deductible contributions in the same or previous years

Refer to Figures 6-1 and 6-2 for examples of Form 8606 and Form 1099-R. Following are a few other things to keep in mind:

■ **Withholding.** Federal income tax is withheld from distributions made from Traditional IRAs unless you choose not to have the tax withheld. How much tax is withheld from an annuity or similar contract is based on your marital status and number of withholding allowances you claim on Form W-4P. If you have not filed the form, the taxes withheld will be as if you are a married and claim three withholding allowances.

■ **Estate tax.** Generally, you must include your IRA assets in your gross estate, to be handled by the executor of your will upon your death. Because each situation requires special handling, consult an attorney or tax accountant.

■ **Penalties**. If you make "no-no" IRA investments and/or prohibited transactions (see Chapter 5), you usually end up paying regular taxes for using your IRA improperly. In some cases, your IRA ceases to be an IRA. Penalties may also apply. These penalties range from a minimum of 6 percent on top of taxes due to 15 percent on the amount of the prohibited transaction, depending upon the specific situation.

CHAPTER 7

MOVING YOUR INVESTMENTS AROUND

You want to both protect the principal amount in your IRA and get the best possible growth of your investments. *Rolling over* your IRA assets from one IRA to another and *transferring* your IRA from one custodian to another are two ways you can do this. Of course, to do so tax-free and penalty-free, you must follow the IRS rules. (In this chapter, all references are to deductible Traditional IRAs unless noted otherwise.)

When you or your IRA's custodian moves your IRA dollars around to maintain the biggest bang for the buck, you have to do so according to the rules; otherwise, somebody loses. Unfortunately, the loser is usually the IRA owner — you. So be sure you understand the IRS rules that apply to your intended IRA rollover or transfer.

Understanding Transfers and Rollovers

An IRA *transfer* involves moving IRA assets from one sponsor, like a bank, to another, like a mutual fund/stock and bond dealer. With an IRA *rollover,* you move your funds out of one IRA (or other investment) and into a new IRA. You can also make rollovers from IRAs to other retirement plans. With rollovers, you take actual possession of your assets in your IRA (or other retirement plan). Table 7-1 compares the transfers and rollovers.

Table 7-1: Comparison of Transfers and Rollovers

Item	Transfer	Rollover
IRA assets	Pass directly from sponsor to sponsor; you do not take possession	Pass *through you,* from account to account
Taxes	None	None on balance if you complete the rollover in 60 days
		Any interest or dividends earned during the 60-day interim period are taxed as income. Sale of securities may result in capital gain or loss.
Frequency	As often as you like	Once during any 12-month period
Reporting	You do not have to report transfers to the IRS	You must report rollovers on your federal tax returns for the years in which they occur
Processing time limit	None, but monitor sponsors to avoid unnecessary delays	Usually immediate because you take possession of assets. Officially, you have 60 days to make the rollover.

If you or a sponsor make a mistake in an IRA transfer or rollover, resulting IRS penalties apply only to that IRA. Keep written copies of all transactions to avoid penalties.

Protecting yourself in a transfer

Following are some things to keep in mind when you transfer IRAs:

- When you make a transfer, the new sponsor usually prepares the necessary documents to complete the transfer. But don't assume that they will. Put your transfer instructions in writing; otherwise, they could be misinterpreted. Keep a copy of this written instruction. It may be useful later if you encounter an unreasonable delay in the transfer.

- Your present IRA sponsor may be in no hurry to complete your transfer. On rare occasions, transfers can be so slow that the sponsor you're transferring from may require a "nudge" from governmental agencies that regulate them.

- Do *not* allow the sponsor from whom you are transferring to give you a check or stock shares to take to the new sponsor. As soon as you take possession of your IRA assets, even for one minute, you are no longer involved in a transfer; you're involved in a rollover (see the following section).

Protecting yourself in a rollover

IRA-to-IRA rollovers have special limitations you need to be aware of so that you don't inadvertently break a rule:

- You can make only one tax-free rollover each year. If you make one on January 15, 2000, you can't make another one with the same IRA until January 15, 2001; otherwise, the IRS treats the second rollover as ordinary income.

- You must rollover the same amount and type of investment from the old IRA to the new IRA.

- You must complete the rollover in 60 days; otherwise, the IRS counts it as income for that year and taxes you for it.

- When making a rollover, don't use any of your IRA assets for something else during the 60-day interim period. When that 60th day rolls around, you must have those assets back in an IRA. The IRS treats any amount *not* back in an IRA as ordinary income, and if you're not yet 59½, the 10-percent early-distribution penalty applies.

Fees You May Encounter

Some investments take time to mature. You should determine what special fees or penalties may be attached to your investments if you move them:

- Certificates of deposit have penalties when you close them before they mature.

- Banks and brokerage houses may have special fees that apply to IRA account moves. You can usually negotiate any fee, especially if your IRA assets have grown to a significant amount of money.

Any IRA trustee fees you are charged are tax deductible, if you pay them with a separate check instead of having them deducted from your IRA balance.

Using Transfers and Rollovers to Build Up Your IRA Investments

You want to tailor your investment strategies to your IRA goals. Generally, what strategy you use depends on your age now and when you will begin withdrawals from your IRAs.

■ Use transfers to move IRAs to sponsors who offer the mix of investments that best match your goals.

■ Use rollovers to increase the balance in an IRA than performs better than others you have.

Rollovers from Traditional IRAs to Roth IRAs

You may rollover a part or all of your Traditional IRA funds to a Roth IRA. You may want to consider this option if you expect to be in a higher tax bracket when you retire. (Chapter 4 has more details about the Roth IRA.)

■ If you make this move, you pay federal taxes on the deductible amount and earnings withdrawn from the Traditional IRA. You do *not* have to pay the 10 percent early withdrawal penalty.

■ To be eligible to convert a Traditional IRA to a Roth IRA, your modified adjusted gross income (MAGI) must be less than $100,000 in the year you convert. To calculate your MAGI, use the worksheet in Table 7-2.

Table 7-2:   Calculating Your MAGI Worksheet

1. Start with your adjusted gross income from IRS Form 1040	$
2. Add any of the following that apply in your case:	$_____
* Foreign earned income exclusion	$_____
* Foreign housing exclusion	$_____
* Interest exclusion on U.S. savings bonds used to pay for higher education	$_____
* Adoption-assistance program exclusions	$_____
* Deduction taken for investments in	

Traditional IRAs	$____
Subtotal	$
3. Subtract the income produced by rolling over or converting a Traditional IRA to a Roth IRA (amount you plan to withdraw from the Traditional IRA, less any non-deductible contributions made to that IRA).	$
Your MAGI	**$**

To determine how much of your Traditional IRA you should convert to a Roth IRA, you can use the Roth Optimizer. Phone 1-877-768-4911 or visit www.rothirabook.com.

Rollovers from employer plans to IRAs

Complicated law governs this type of rollover. These laws concern timing, how much of the retirement plan is your money, and whether you prefer a full or partial rollover. Generally, the IRS allows a tax-free rollover lump-sum distribution from an employer plan for the following reasons:

■ You leave your job.

■ Your employer drops a pension plan or permanently ceases paying into a qualified employee plan and pays you your entire share.

■ You are 59½ or older.

■ You die, your spouse is your beneficiary, and he or she decides to roll your inherited benefits from the employer plan into an IRA.

■ You divorce and the settlement calls for such a rollover.

Because rollovers to IRAs from other retirement plans can be so complex, get professional advice about your individual circumstances.

General rules regarding moving assets

When you perform a rollover or transfer, keep these rules in mind:

■ You cannot mix assets when transferring or making a rollover from one retirement account to another.

■ If you transfer an IRA to another custodian, you must transfer it as is. When the IRA is invested in stocks, for example, you have to transfer it as stocks.

■ When you rollover cash or other assets, you must either roll over the actual cash distributed or sell other assets (like securities) and roll over the proceeds.

■ If you sell the distributed property and rollover all the proceeds, sale proceeds (including any portion representing an increase in value) are treated as part of the distribution and are not included in your gross income.

Remember

If you rollover only part of the proceeds, you are taxed on the part you keep. You must allocate the part you keep between its value upon distribution and its change in value due to its sale. The chart in Table 7-3 shows an example scenario.

Table 7-3: How Much of Your Gain Is Taxed

	Item	Amount
A	Charles receives an eligible rollover distribution of $50,000 in non-employer stock from his employer's non-contributory retirement plan	$50,000
B	Charles sells the stock for $60,000, making a net gain of $10,000	+ $10,000
C	Value of stock	$60,000
	Charles rolls over $45,000 of the $60,000 proceeds from the sale into his IRA	- $45,000
D	What's left over (which includes part of the gain from the sale of his stock)	$15,000

Item	Amount
Amount Charles reports as capital gains (B ÷ C x D)	$2,500
Amount Charles reports as ordinary income (A ÷ C x D)	$12,000

Table 7-4 shows another scenario that is similar to the preceding except that Charles loses money on the sale of his stocks.

Table 7-4:   How Much of Your Loss Is Taxed

	Item	Amount
A	Charles receives an eligible rollover distribution of $50,000 in non-employer stock from his employer's non-contributory retirement plan	$50,000
B	Charles sells the stock for $40,000, resulting in a loss of $10,000	- $10,000
C	Value of stock	$40,000
	Charles rolls over $25,000 of the $40,000 proceeds from the sale into his IRA	- $25,000
D	What's left over (which includes part of the gain from the sale of his stock)	$15,000
	Amount Charles reports as capital loss (B ÷ C x D)	$3,750
	Amount Charles reports as ordinary income (A ÷ C x D)	$18,750

CHAPTER 8

IRAS AND THE THREE DS

- Handling options and distributions on inherited IRAs
- Dividing IRA assets in a divorce
- Understanding IRS disability guidelines
- Filling out the right IRS form if you make a mistake

When it comes to handling IRAs when they are inherited, part of a divorce settlement, or affected by other extraordinary events, it's important to get good advice. In these circumstances, consult with a CPA, lawyer, or trusted banker who can help you figure out the appropriate plan of action.

You especially want to get good advice when these events happen after many years of IRA investing, when assets amount to a significant sum.

IRAs and Death

When the owner an IRA begins an account, he or she names a beneficiary (or beneficiaries), who will inherit the account in the event that the owner dies. What the beneficiary can do with the account — whether the beneficiary has to begin (or continue) distributions, and so on — depends on whether the beneficiary is a spouse or someone else and what type of IRA is being inherited.

Inheriting a Traditional IRA

If you are the surviving spouse and sole beneficiary of a Traditional IRA, and your spouse dies before all assets of the account are distributed, you automatically inherit the IRA and can do the following:

■ Make contributions to the inherited IRA

■ Make rollovers into the inherited IRA

■ Rollover the assets, tax-free, into a new Traditional IRA that you become the owner of. This new account is not subject to any distribution requirements of the "old" IRA (the one owned by your deceased spouse).

If your aren't yet 70½, rolling over the old IRA into a new IRA is the best move.

■ If you elect not to treat the inherited IRA as your own, you must begin distributions from the inherited IRA; see Table 8-1 for rules regarding when these distributions should begin.

Table 8-1:   Distributions on Inherited IRAs

Beneficiary	*Situation*	*Distribution Rules*
Spouse	You don't rollover IRA into a new account	Distributions must begin by later of
		Dec. 31 of year deceased spouse would have reached 70½
		Dec. 31 of year following spouse's death
	You rollover IRA into new account you own	Former distribution rules don't apply

Non-spouse	Distributions had begun by owner's death	Remaining funds must be distributed as quickly as they had been up to the owner's death
	Distributions had not begun at time of death	All funds must be distributed as follows: Begin by Dec. 31 of year following owner's death Continue over the life of the designated beneficiary
Multiple beneficiaries	Distributions had begun by owner's death	Remaining funds must be distributed as quickly as they had been up to the owner's death
	Distributions had not begun at time of death	All funds must be distributed as follows: Begin by Dec. 31 of year following owner's death Continue over a period not extending beyond the life expectancy of the beneficiary with the shortest life expectancy

You must calculate minimum distribution amounts annually, based upon your continued life expectancy.

IRS publications 590 and 939 contain life expectancy tables giving applicable divisors for figuring required minimum distributions. Also, Publication 590's Appendix A, "Summary

Record of Traditional IRA9(s) for 1998," includes a worksheet for determining required annual distributions from
your Traditional IRA(s) (see Figure 8-1).

Figure 8-1:   Worksheet for figuring out your required annual distributions.

WORKSHEET
FOR
DETERMINING REQUIRED ANNUAL DISTRIBUTIONS FROM YOUR IRA(s)

	70½	71½	72½	73½	74½	75½
1. Age						
2. Year age was reached						
3. Value of IRA at the close of business on December 31 of the year immediately prior to the year on line 2[1]						
4. Divisor from Life Expectancy Table I or Table II[2]						
5. Required distribution (divide line 3 by line 4)[3]						

[1]If you have more than one IRA, you must figure the required distribution separately for each IRA.

[2]Use the appropriate divisor for each year and for each IRA. You can either (a) use the appropriate divisor from the table each year, or (b) use the appropriate divisor from the table for your 70½ year and reduce it by 1 (one) for each subsequent year. To find the appropriate divisor, use your age (and that of your beneficiary, if applicable) as of your birthday(s) in the year shown on line 2. If your beneficiary is someone other than your spouse, see *Minimum Distribution Incidental Benefit Requirement* in Chapter 5.

[3]If you have more than one IRA, you must withdraw an amount equal to the total of the required distributions figured for each IRA. You can, however, withdraw the total from one IRA or from more than one IRA.

When the owner of a Traditional IRA dies and the beneficiary
is someone other than the surviving spouse or there is more
than one beneficiary, the situation becomes more complex:

■ The Traditional IRA becomes part of the deceased's
   estate.

■ Generally, taxes are not owed on assets in the IRA until
   distributions are made from it.

■ You must make distributions. Refer to Table 8-1.

Inheriting a Roth IRA

If a Roth IRA owner dies, certain minimum distribution rules
that apply to Traditional IRAs apply to Roth IRAs, even
though the Roth IRA owner was not required to take any distributions. Refer to Table 8-1.

Generally, all the assets in the Roth IRA must be distributed
by the end of the fifth calendar year after the year of the
owner's death, unless the assets are payable to a designated
beneficiary over that beneficiary's lifetime.

■ If the distribution is paid as an annuity (a yearly allotment) to the designated beneficiary, it must be payable over the beneficiary's life expectancy. Distributions must begin before the end of the calendar year following the year of the owner's death.

■ If the sole beneficiary is the spouse, he or she can either delay distributions until the decedent would have reached age 70½, or treat the Roth IRA as his or her own IRA.

Beneficiaries of Roth IRAs generally receive distributions tax-free, provided the distributions meet requirements for qualified distributions (refer to Chapter 4). Also, tax-free qualifications may be limited. If you find yourself in this situation, consult an expert.

If you are the beneficiary, you must be careful not to mix or substitute required distributions from IRAs you inherit. You must figure minimum distribution amounts separately for each IRA. Follow these two rules:

■ Don't use distributions from Traditional IRAs for required distributions from Roth IRAs.

■ Unless multiple Roth IRAs were inherited from the same person, you must figure distributions from each Roth IRA separately.

Education IRAs

Education IRAs are not retirement accounts, but educational trust funds. There is no "owner" of an Education IRA other than its designated beneficiary. If this beneficiary dies before all assets are distributed, another qualified beneficiary (member of the decedent's family) can be named. All the rules that applied to the former beneficiary apply to the new one.

IRAs and Divorce

You don't have to liquidate IRA assets during a divorce; instead you can divide them. By doing so correctly, you can avoid paying taxes on the transfer.

Traditional and Roth IRAs

If you get divorced or legally separated, you can transfer all or part of a Traditional IRA or Roth IRA tax-free to your spouse or former spouse. The part of the IRA that is transferred is treated as your former spouse's IRA from the date of the transfer. Similarly, your spouse can transfer his or her IRA to you, in which case it becomes your property.

In either case, you can accomplish the transfer with either of the following two commonly used methods:

■ Change the name on the IRA from one spouse to the other.

■ Make a direct transfer of IRA assets by directing the custodian of the original IRA to transfer the affected assets to the custodian of a new or existing IRA in the name of the spouse or former spouse. Any remaining assets in the original IRA can be left intact.

Employer plan distribution

If, in a divorce, you receive a distribution from your spouse's or former spouse's employer plan, you can roll over all or part of the distribution into a Traditional IRA, tax-free, if both of the following conditions are met:

■ The distribution would have been an eligible rollover to the employee.

■ The rollover was made under a *Qualified Domestic Relations Order*, which gives an alternate payee the right to receive all or part of the benefits that would be payable to a participant under the plan.

Education IRAs

If a child, as a beneficiary of an Education IRA, transfers his or her assets to a former spouse in a divorce situation, the transfer is not taxed. Also, the former spouse is then the designated beneficiary of the Education IRA.

IRAs and Disability

Disability is one of the qualifiers that exempts Traditional IRA and Roth IRA owners from certain rules governing withdrawals from their accounts. You are considered disabled if

■ You provide proof that you cannot do any substantial gainful activity because of your physical or mental condition.

■ A physician determines that your condition can be expected to result in death or to be of long, continued, and indefinite duration.

■ A physician certifies in writing that the condition has lasted or can be expected to last continuously for 12 months or more.

Being laid up with a broken leg or even long-term post-surgical recovery doesn't qualify as disability.

If you become disabled before you reach 59½, any amounts you withdraw from your Traditional IRA because of your disability are not subject to the 10 percent additional tax. However, you must satisfy IRS requirements to qualify as disabled and file Schedule R (Form 1040) or Schedule 3 (Form 1040A) with your return for each tax year you are disabled. You don't need to submit the physician's certification with your return, but keep this document with your own tax records.

Getting Help If You Make a Mistake

The IRS has a form for everything, and Form 5329 is no exception to this rule (see Figure 8-2). Unlike most IRS forms, however, Form 5329 can be a relief for taxpayers, especially those who suddenly become IRA owners through inheritance or divorce and make a mistake regarding distribution requirements. If, for example, you failed to withdraw the minimum required through a reasonable error, the IRS may excuse you from the 50 percent excise tax for that year on the amount that wasn't distributed as it should have been.

Figure 8–2: IRS Form 5329.

Form **5329**	Additional Taxes Attributable to IRAs, Other Qualified Retirement Plans, Annuities, Modified Endowment Contracts, and MSAs	OMB No. 1545-0203
Department of the Treasury Internal Revenue Service	(Under Sections 72, 530, 4973, and 4974 of the Internal Revenue Code) ▶ Attach to Form 1040. See separate instructions.	19**98** Attachment Sequence No. **29**

Name of individual subject to additional tax. (If married filing jointly, see page 2 of the instructions.)		Your social security number
Fill in Your Address Only If You Are Filing This Form by Itself and Not With Your Tax Return	Home address (number and street), or P.O. box if mail is not delivered to your home	Apt. no.
	City, town or post office, state, and ZIP code	If this is an amended return, check here ▶ ☐

If you are subject to the 10% tax on early distributions **only,** see **Who Must File** in the instructions before continuing. You may be able to report this tax directly on Form 1040 without filing Form 5329.

Part I   Tax on Early Distributions

Complete this part if a taxable distribution was made from your qualified retirement plan (including an IRA other than an education (Ed) IRA), annuity contract, or modified endowment contract before you reached age 59 ½ (or was incorrectly indicated as such on your Form 1099-R–see instructions). **Note:** You must include the amount of the distribution on line 15b or 16b of Form 1040.

1	Early distributions included in gross income (see page 3 of the instructions)	**1**	
2	Distributions excepted from additional tax (see page 3 of the instructions). Enter appropriate exception number from instructions ▶ _____	**2**	
3	Amount subject to additional tax. Subtract line 2 from line 1	**3**	
4	**Tax due.** Multiply line 3 by 10% (.10). Enter here and on Form 1040, line 53	**4**	
	Caution: If any amount on line 3 was a distribution from a SIMPLE retirement plan, you must multiply that distribution by 25% (.25) instead of 10%. See instructions for more information.		

Part II   Tax on Distributions From Ed IRAs Not Used for Educational Expenses

Complete this part if a distribution was made from your Ed IRA and was not used for educational expenses.
Note: You must include the amount of the distribution on line 15b of Form 1040.

5	Taxable amount from line 29 of Form 8606	**5**	
6	Distributions excepted from additional tax (see page 4 of the instructions)	**6**	
7	Amount subject to additional tax. Subtract line 6 from line 5	**7**	
8	**Tax due.** Multiply line 7 by 10% (.10). Enter here and on Form 1040, line 53	**8**	

Part III   Tax on Excess Contributions to Traditional IRAs

Complete this part if, either in this year or in earlier years, you contributed more to your traditional IRAs than is or was allowable and you have an excess contribution subject to tax.

9	Excess contributions for 1998 (see page 4 of the instructions). Do not include this amount on Form 1040, line 23		**9**	
10	Earlier year excess contributions not previously eliminated (see page 4 of the instructions)	**10**		
11	Contribution credit. If your actual contribution for 1998 is less than your maximum allowable contribution, see page 4 of the instructions; otherwise, enter -0-	**11**		
12	1998 distributions from your traditional IRA accounts that are includible in taxable income	**12**		
13	1997 tax year excess contributions (if any) withdrawn after the due date (including extensions) of your 1997 income tax return, and 1996 and earlier tax year excess contributions withdrawn in 1998	**13**		
14	Add lines 11, 12, and 13	**14**		
15	Adjusted earlier year excess contributions. Subtract line 14 from line 10. Enter the result, but not less than zero		**15**	
16	Total excess contributions. Add lines 9 and 15		**16**	
17	**Tax due.** Enter the **smaller** of 6% (.06) of line 16 or 6% (.06) of the value of your traditional IRAs on the last day of 1998. Also enter this amount on Form 1040, line 53		**17**	

Part IV   Tax on Excess Contributions to Roth IRAs

18	Excess contributions for 1998 (see page 5 of the instructions)	**18**	
19	**Tax due.** Enter the **smaller** of 6% (.06) of line 18 or 6% (.06) of the value of your Roth IRAs on the last day of 1998. Also enter this amount on Form 1040, line 53	**19**	

For Paperwork Reduction Act Notice, see page 6 of separate instructions.	Cat. No. 13329Q	Form **5329** (1998)

Figure 8-3:   IRS Form 5329, *continued*

Form 5329 (1998)   Page **2**

	Part V Tax on Excess Contributions to Ed IRAs			

20	Excess contributions for 1998 (see page 5 of the instructions).	**20**	
21	**Tax due.** Enter the **smaller** of 6% (.06) of line 20 or 6% (.06) of the value of your Ed IRAs on the last day of 1998. Also enter this amount on Form 1040, line 53	**21**	

	Part VI Tax on Excess Contributions to Medical Savings Accounts (MSAs)		

Complete this part if, either in 1998 or 1997, you or your employer contributed more to your MSAs than is or was allowable and you have an excess contribution subject to tax.

22	Excess contributions for 1998 (see page 5 of the instructions). Do not include this amount on Form 1040, line 25		**22**	
23	1997 excess contributions not previously eliminated (see page 5 of the instructions)	**23**		
24	Contribution credit. If your actual contribution for 1998 is less than your maximum allowable contribution, see page 6 of the instructions; otherwise, enter -0-	**24**		
25	1998 distributions from your MSA account(s) that are includible in taxable income	**25**		
26	1997 tax year excess contributions (if any) withdrawn in 1998 after the due date (including extensions) of your 1997 income tax return	**26**		
27	Add lines 24, 25, and 26	**27**		
28	Adjusted 1997 excess contributions. Subtract line 27 from line 23. Enter the result, but not less than zero		**28**	
29	Total excess contributions. Add lines 22 and 28		**29**	
30	**Tax due.** Enter the **smaller** of 6% (.06) of line 29 or 6% (.06) of the value of your MSAs on the last day of 1998. Also enter this amount on Form 1040, line 53		**30**	

	Part VII Tax on Excess Accumulation in Qualified Retirement Plans		

Complete this part if you did not receive the minimum required distribution from your qualified retirement plan (including an IRA other than an Ed IRA or Roth IRA).

31	Minimum required distribution (see page 6 of the instructions)	**31**	
32	Amount actually distributed to you	**32**	
33	Subtract line 32 from line 31. If line 32 is more than line 31, enter -0-	**33**	
34	**Tax due.** Multiply line 33 by 50% (.50). Enter here and on Form 1040, line 53	**34**	

Signature. Complete *ONLY* if you are filing this form by itself and not with your tax return.

Please Sign Here	Under penalties of perjury, I declare that I have examined this form, including accompanying schedules and statements, and to the best of my knowledge and belief, it is true, correct, and complete. Declaration of preparer (other than taxpayer) is based on all information of which preparer has any knowledge.		
	▶ Your signature		▶ Date
Paid Preparer's Use Only	Preparer's signature ▶	Date	Check if self-employed ▶ ☐ Preparer's social security no.
	Firm's name (or yours, if self-employed) and address ▶		EIN ▶
			ZIP code ▶

To file a request to excuse the tax:

1. File Form 5329 (Part VII) with your Form 1040, entering the amount of tax, and pay that tax.

2. Attach an explanation for the excess accumulation, showing when you removed the excess and what you have done that will result in its withdrawal.

If the IRS approves your request, it refunds the excess accumulations tax you paid.

CHAPTER 9

WEATHERING TOUGH ECONOMIC CONDITIONS

IN THIS CHAPTER

- Understanding how you can best protect your investments from inflation

- Knowing the ramifications of missing or skipping contributions

- Avoiding penalties for excessive and nondeductible contributions.

This book can't give you assurances that your investments will always perform splendidly. However, it can supply you with useful information that can help you weather future economic storms.

Handling Inflation

Economists and others have been scaring investors with predictions that inflation is hiding around the corner, just waiting to come back. As you build your retirement, you do need to be concerned about the effect of inflation on your savings. Table 9-1 shows how various rates of inflation can erode the buying power of $10,000 over a period of years. (*Note:* This table uses a base amount of $10,000 today.)

Table 9-1:   What $10,000 Will Be Worth Years From Now

Future Years	2% inflation	4% inflation	6% inflation
5	$9,057	$8,219	$7,473
10	$8,203	$6,756	$5,584
15	$7,430	$5,553	$4,173
20	$6,730	$4,564	$3,118

Even at 4 percent, inflation can cut buying power by one-third in a decade.

You want to guard your long-term IRA investments against inflation's erosion of buying power. The best way to adjust for inflation is to do your best in making investments that outpace it. For example, if inflation is growing at 3 percent annually, seek investments that are expected to grow at 5 to 6 percent annually. Chapter 5 contains details about investment strategies.

If you're worried about inflation, watch monthly wholesale prices and the monthly consumer price index. If these continue to grow from month to month, that could trigger a rise in inflation. You can monitor these prices at the U.S. Bureau of Labor Statistics at the following Web sites:

- `http://stats.bls.gov/cpihome.htm`
- `http://stats.bls.gov/ppihome.htm`

One way to help protect yourself against inflation is to diversify your IRA investments to include those that outpace or at least keep up with inflation.

Investing in real estate

If your IRA assets are in the six-figure range, you and your financial advisors may want to take a look at Real Estate Investment Trusts, called (REITs). These trusts own apartments, office buildings, shopping centers, and other types of real estate. Like mutual funds, they sell shares to investors.

REITs can be high-yielding investments, sometimes paying double or triple the average dividend on Dow Jones industrial stocks. For example, in 1992 when the average Dow stock yielded around 3 percent, REITs like Federal Realty Investment Trust and others had yields between 6 and 7 percent.

You buy shares in publicly traded REITs the same way you buy any stock, through a broker.

Younger people who have years to go before they retire and who have a higher tolerance for risk may want to invest in REITS. Others — for example, those who are closer to retirement or who have a low risk threshold — probably should pursue other investment options. Consult a financial advisor if you're interested in REITs.

"Stay short" when rates are low

Many IRA owners have a portion of their investments in the tried-and-true insured deposits with financial institutions like banks, savings associations, and credit unions.

Compound interest and dividend rates paid on time deposits like CDs are lower when inflation is lower, usually staying ahead of inflation by several points. In this situation, you want to "stay short," with investments that mature anywhere from three or six months to one and 2½ years at most.

When inflation begins to rise, your best long-term defense against its erosion is to shift more of your investment power into stocks and mutual funds, which have managed to gain an annual average of 10.4 percent since 1926 — comfortably ahead of the 3.1 percent inflation average over the same long-term. When your CDs are about to mature, their depository institution generally notifies you by mail. In this notification, the institution does the following:

- Stipulates that the investment will be automatically renewed when it matures, unless you decide otherwise.

- States the interest or dividend rate at renewal.

- Provides for a grace period during which you can reinvest the principal and accumulated earnings as you like.

If economic conditions haven't changed since you originally bought the CD, and the new rate is the same as or higher than the former rate, you probably want to renew. (You also can put the money in a more aggressive investment. See Chapter 4 to find out about IRA investment options.) To go online for information about which banks offer the best CDs in the nation, visit the Wall Street Journal at www.wsj.com.

If you choose to move these funds from their present custodian institution, you'll be involved in a once-a-year rollover. See Chapter 7 of this book about IRA rollovers and transfers.

Making Irregular Contributions

Regardless of what the economy in general is doing, you may experience tough economic times: loss of a job, for example, or a major illness that takes you away from work for an extended period of time. Priorities for taking care of basic needs during tough times may put saving for retirement on hold. Usually, these circumstances are only temporary.

Skipped or missed contributions

Having a tough time making ends meet may prevent you from keeping up with your regular IRA contributions. Don't lose sleep over the fact that you either temporarily — or even permanently — can't find the dollars to continue IRA contributions:

■ You face no penalty for interrupting the flow of IRA contributions — other than the lost opportunity to sock away more tax-advantaged dollars for retirement.

■ All IRAs continue to compound their earnings tax-free even when you don't make contributions.

Table 9-2 shows three investors, A, B, and C, who each have IRAs earning 10 percent a year, and what effect missed or prematurely stopped contributions have on their IRAs at retirement.

Table 9-2: The Effect of Missed Contributions

	Yearly contribution	Situation	Growth Funds at Retirement
A	$2,000 for 7 yrs.	Stops making contributions at 25 and leaves IRA to compound interest until 65	944,641 (including the $14,000 contribution) 66-fold growth
B	$2,000 for 5 years	Stops making contributions at 18 and leaves IRA to compound interest until 65	$1,184,600 117-fold growth (including the $10,000 contribution)
C	>$2,000 for 6 yrs	Stops making contributions at 13 and leaves IRA to compound interest until 65	$1,272,930 188-fold growth (including the $6,750 contribution)

Although these scenarios are fairly optimistic (after all, not many people begin making contributions at 13 years of age), they do illustrate that missing contributions need not way-lay your retirement plans. The key to successfully building retirement income is to start as early as you can (whether that's at 30, 40, or 50 years of age) and to contribute as much as you can. Remember, you can only do the best you can do.

Excessive contributions

If you ever contribute more than you should to your IRA (or IRAs) in a given year ($2,000 maximum for an individual; $4,000 maximum for joint filers), you may have to pay a tax on the excess contribution.

One way excessive contributions happen is when a Traditional IRA owner gets an unexpected boost in income, like a bonus, that drives his or her modified adjusted gross income (MAGI) over the maximum allowed ($150,000 for joint filers) for qualified contributions. Such an event automatically changes the IRA contribution for that year from fully deductible to partly deductible.

If you exceed the maximum IRA contribution, and you don't do anything to change it before you file your tax return for that year, the IRS treats this as an excessive contribution and views the non-deductible amount as a distribution from that IRA.

If you act fast after an excessive contribution, you can withdraw the excess amount so that it is not taxed as a distribution. Follow these steps:

1. Withdraw the excess contribution and any income earned on the excess amount by the due date (including extensions) of your tax return for that year.

2. Do *not* claim a deduction for the amount of the contribution withdrawn.

3. Include on your Form 1040 the *income earned* on the contributions withdrawn, along with an explanation.

4. If you weren't yet 59½ at the time, file Form 5329, Part 1, to report the *income earned* as an early withdrawal. If you do this, *do not* include the withdrawn contribution as an excess contribution on Form 5329. (See Chapter 8 of this book for a sample of Form 5329.)

When you make excess contributions to a Roth IRA or an Education IRA, you follow the same steps to avoid taxation as a distribution.

Non-deductible contributions

When you make non-deductible contributions to a Traditional IRA either in combination with deductible contributions or simply by themselves, you have to follow these rules:

■ You can make any combination of deductible and non-deductible annual contributions up to the maximum limits ($2,000 for individuals; $4,000 for joint filers).

■ To figure what parts of your annual contributions are deductible and non-deductible, use the Worksheet for Reduced IRA Deduction. You can get this worksheet from the IRS (www.irs.gov).

■ Non-deductible contributions to your IRA are taxable. Because you've already paid taxes on these amounts when you made your contribution, you can withdraw them tax-free. That's why it's important to keep accurate records of both deductible and non-deductible IRA contributions.

■ You can use a record-keeping worksheet to keep track of your deductible and non-deductible IRA contributions (see Figure 9-1).

Figure 9-1:   Summary Record of IRA(s)

APPENDIX A. Summary Record of IRA(s) for 1997 (You May Keep This for Your Records.)

Name _____

I was ☐ covered ☐ not covered by my employer's retirement plan during the year.

I became age 59½ on _____
                     (month) (day) (year)

I became age 70½ on _____
                     (month) (day) (year)

Contributions

Name of IRA	Date	Amount contributed for 1997	Check, if rollover contribution	Fair Market value of IRA as of December 31, 1997, from Form 5498
1.				
2.				
3.				
4.				
5.				
Total				

Total contributions deducted on tax return $ _____

Total contributions treated as nondeductible on Form 8606 $ _____

Distributions

Name of IRA	Date	Amount of distribution	Reason (e.g., for retirement, rollover, withdrawal of excess contributions, etc.)	Income earned on IRA	Taxable amount reported on income tax return	Nontaxable amount from Form 8606, line 10
1.						
2.						
3.						
4.						
Total						

Basis of all IRAs as of 12/31/97 (from Form 8606, line 11) $ _____

Basis of all IRAs for 1997 (from Form 8606, line 12) $ _____

Note: *You should keep copies of your income tax return, and Forms W-2, 8606, and 5498.*

WORKSHEET
FOR
DETERMINING REQUIRED ANNUAL DISTRIBUTIONS FROM YOUR IRA(s)

	70½	71½	72½	73½	74½	75½
1. Age						
2. Year age was reached						
3. Value of IRA at the close of business on December 31 of the year immediately prior to the year on line 2[1]						
4. Divisor from Life Expectancy Table I or Table II[2]						
5. Required distribution (divide line 3 by line 4)[3]						

[1]If you have more than one IRA, you must figure the required distribution separately for each IRA.

[2]Use the appropriate divisor for each year and for each IRA. You can either (a) use the appropriate divisor from the table each year, or (b) use the appropriate divisor from the table for your 70½ year and reduce it by 1 (one) for each subsequent year. To find the appropriate divisor, use your age (and that of your beneficiary, if applicable) as of your birthday(s) in the year shown on line 2. If your beneficiary is someone other than your spouse, see *Minimum Distribution Incidental Benefit Requirement* in Chapter 5.

[3]If you have more than one IRA, you must withdraw an amount equal to the total of the required distributions figured for each IRA. You can, however, withdraw the total from one IRA or from more than one IRA.

■   When you file your tax return for any year in which you make non-deductible contributions, you must also file Form 8606 "Nondeductible IRAs" (see Chapter 6 for an example of this form). You must file this form even if you do not have to file a tax return for that year.

Following are a few important points to remember:

- If you do not report nondeductible contributions, all of your Traditional IRA contributions are treated as deductible, which means that, when you make withdrawals, the amounts withdrawn will be taxed. The only way to avoid this tax is to prove, with satisfactory evidence, that you actually made nondeductible contributions.

- If you don't file Form 8606, you have to pay a $50 penalty every time you fail to do so, unless you can prove your failure was due to reasonable cause.

- If you overstate the amount of your non-deductible contributions on Form 8606 for any tax year, you must pay a penalty of $100, again unless you can prove it was due to reasonable cause.

CHAPTER 10

REAPING THE HARVEST

The federal government created IRAs to give taxpayers an incentive for saving toward their retirement and other long-term goals. You are expected to use these savings accordingly.

When the time comes to receive regular distributions from your IRA or IRAs, you should plan these only as part of your retirement income. To fully enjoy the fruits of your dedicated commitment over the years, you have to make some plans and decisions.

Receiving Distributions

When you turn 59½, you can begin taking distributions from your Traditional IRA without penalty. If possible — that is, you are not disabled and still have earned income — you may want to consider leaving your IRA assets intact so that they can continue to compound.

Keep in mind, however, that you cannot keep funds in a Traditional IRA indefinitely. Eventually you must withdraw them. If you haven't already, you must begin withdrawals when you turn 70½. (This rule does not apply to Roth IRAs.)

If you do not make any withdrawals from a Traditional IRA or if you do not withdraw enough, you may have to pay a 50-percent excise tax on the amount not withdrawn.

You can withdraw the balance of a Traditional IRA account in one of two ways:

■ Withdraw the entire balance by April 1 following the year in which you reach 70½. (Just add six months to your birthday and circle April 1st of the next year.)

■ Begin withdrawal of incremental distributions by the same deadline and then receive the required minimum distribution for every year thereafter by December 31.

Table 10-1:   When You Must Make Withdrawals from Traditional IRAs

Type of Withdrawal	You Reach 70½ On	First Withdrawal By	Subsequent Required Min. Distribution By
Incremental, Minimum Required Distributions	Aug. 20, 2000	April 1, 2001	December 31, 2001 and every year thereafter by Dec. 31st
Lump-sum	Aug. 20, 2000	April 1, 2001	N/A

If you're making incremental distributions, you can avoid paying taxes on two distributions in one year by not waiting until the last minute to begin your withdrawals. If you begin incremental withdrawals in December of your 69th year, you don't have to make another withdrawal until the following December.

Warning

Avoid premature distributions. Early distributions kick the dollars withdrawn into the category of gross income. The amount withdrawn is taxable in the year withdrawn. Added to that is a 10 percent tax penalty on the amount withdrawn. There are a few exceptions to this rule about premature distributions. Refer to Chapter 8 for details.

Lump Sum versus Incremental Distributions

If you're like most people, you will probably retire, at least partially, by your late 60's. When IRAs are among the assets you own, consider your options for enjoying their benefits during retirement.

Lump sum

If you elect the lump sum distribution, you can rollover the entire IRA to purchase an annuity from an insurance company:

- The insurance company makes regular, fixed-amount payments to you over your remaining lifetime.

- These payments are taxed as ordinary income when you receive them.

- When you die, the value of any annuities you have generally passes to named beneficiaries or to your gross estate.

You can also rollover part or all of your Traditional IRA or IRAs to a Roth IRA before your 70½ deadline. This is a wise option if:

- You don't really need your Traditional IRA assets to make ends meet for the next five years, and you can afford to pay the taxes now on the amount you convert to the

Roth IRA. (**Note:** You don't have to convert the entire balance. Have a CPA calculate the tax consequences before you do this.)

■ You don't want to be bothered with figuring minimum required distributions each year, which Roth IRA withdrawals do not require.

■ You prefer to continue contributions beyond 70½, which you can only do with a Roth IRA.

■ You want to leave some IRA assets to your heirs and you want the most favorable post-death distribution of your IRA assets, which the Roth IRA allows. These assets are free of estate taxes and pass to beneficiaries tax-free.

Because you have to pay taxes on Traditional IRA withdrawals anyway, rolling them over to a Roth IRA continues the tax-free growth of these assets. You may decide that doing so is preferable to paying taxes on the entire lump sum Traditional IRA distribution.

You can find additional details about rollovers in Chapter 7.

Incremental

When you choose the incremental, or periodic, distribution option, you can make withdrawals in a series of installments (monthly, quarterly, and so on) as long as the total distributions for the year equal the minimum required amount.

To figure the minimum required amount, you must determine your life expectancy. Do so by using Tables I and II in Appendix E of IRS Publication 590 and the tables in IRS Publication 939. These documents are free for the asking (visit www.irs.gov or see the Resource section in back of this book).

Applicable life expectancy is one of the following:

■ Single life expectancy of you as the IRA owner

■ Joint life expectancy of you owner and your designated IRA beneficiary

■ The remaining life expectancy of the designated beneficiary or beneficiaries (if you die before distributions have begun)

Be sure to use the correct table for your situation. Because life expectancy decreases with each year, you must refigure minimum required distribution each year.

Consider this example: Pete, born October 1, 1927, reaches 70½ in 1998. Sarah, his wife and beneficiary, turns 56 in September 1998. Pete begins receiving distributions on April 1, 1999. Pete's IRA account balance as of December 31, 1997 was $29,000 (preceding year's balance). Based on their ages at year-end (12/31/98), the joint life expectancy for Pete and Sarah is 29 years (Table II, Appendix E). Table 10-2 shows how Pete's minimum distribution is figured.

Table 10-2:   Example: Figuring Minimum Distribution

Item	Amount	Explanation	Distribution Date
Beginning 12/31/97 balance	$29,000		
Required minimum distribution for 1998 (1st distribution year)	$1,000	$29,000 ÷29 (life expectancy)	Distributed 4/1/99
Balance on 12/31/98	$29,680	Remember, because the money is still in the account, it continues to earn interest	

Required minimum distribution for 1999 (2nd distribution year)	$1017	Distributed 12/31/99

If you have a beneficiary other than your spouse who is more than 10 years younger than you, additional steps are required for figuring your required minimum distribution. These steps are outlined in IRS Publication 590.

Here are some important things to remember about required minimum distributions:

■ They are minimums. You can withdraw more than the minimum.

■ The more you withdraw over and above the minimum, the more you reduce the continued compound earning power of your IRA. Also, you do not receive credit for the additional amount when figuring required minimums for future years.

■ You must refigure the required minimum each year. Use the balance in the IRA as of December 31 of the preceding year (minus any above minimum withdrawals that year).

■ If you fail to make a withdrawal during any required year, you may have to pay a 50 percent excise tax on the amount not distributed.

■ If your spouse is your sole IRA beneficiary and dies before you do, his or her life expectancy becomes zero in the next calendar year.

Getting the greatest monetary rewards

To get the greatest rewards from your IRA distributions, do the following:

- Plan distributions in advance, to coincide with other retirement income.

- Discuss your plans for IRA distributions with at least one other person and write these plans down. This person should be your trusted financial advisor, CPA, or banker.

- Be sure you understand the reporting requirements for distributions and the federal tax forms required for these. If you can, consult a CPA or other expert. Otherwise, go to the local library and read IRS guidelines.

- If you have made any non-deductible contributions to a Traditional IRA, you must use an IRS worksheet to figure the taxable part of each distribution, and then you file Form 8606 for each year until you run out of cost basis equal to the amount of your non-deductible contributions. "Cost basis" is an accounting term that in the case of Traditional IRAs refers to the original value of non-deductible contributions.

- If you converted any Traditional IRA assets to a Roth IRA, don't touch the Roth IRAs assets until you have exhausted the assets in your Traditional IRAs. Tapping Traditional IRA assets first reduces the size of your taxable estate. Also, remember you must take care to observe the Roth IRA first 5-year rule before tax-free withdrawals can be made (for more information about Roth IRA features, refer to Chapter 4).

Living on Your Distributions During Retirement

Neither your Social Security benefits nor your IRA distributions alone are likely to cover all your retirement costs of living. Sources of income for your retirement may include all or most of the following:

- Social Security benefits (estimated to equal no more than 20 to 30 percent of your pre-retirement gross income)

- Income from any employment during your retirement

- Pensions and annuity benefits

- Dividends and interest from other income and investments

- Tax-advantaged assets, including benefits from IRAs and employer plans, such as 401(k)s

2Assets from IRA and similar plans are ideally left as your final resource for retirement income.

If you can project your retirement income needs as outlined in Chapter 2, you can estimate what you will need to withdraw from IRAs and other tax-advantaged assets each year of retirement. To figure out how much you need to withdraw, determine how much you need each month (adjusting for inflation) and then subtract this amount from what you expect to receive from your income sources. The result is what you need from your IRA each month. Table 10-3 shows an example in which the IRA owner needs $2,083 per month during his first year of retirement and has $100,000 in his IRA upon retirement.

Table 10-3: Sample Retirement Capital Projection Sheet

	Income Sources					Present	Revised
Age	Needed per mo. @ 3%	Soc Sec incr. @ 2%	Pension	Other income or (Exp)	Surplus or (shortage) per mo.	$100,000 plus plus $0 per mo.@ 8%	$100,000 plus $0 per mo. @ 9%
65	2,083	1,000	1,000		(83)	106,920	107,910
66	2,146	1,020	1,000		(126)	113,843	115,976
67	2,210	1,040	1,000		(170)	120,750	124,193
68	2,277	1,061	1,000		(215)	112,7619	132,554
69	2,345	1,082	1,000		(262)	134,428	141,052
70	2,415	1,104	1,000		(311)	141,151	149,678
71	2,488	1,126	1,000		(361)	147,759	158,421
72	2,562	1,149	1,000		(414)	154,220	167,270
73	2,639	1,172	1,000		(467)	160,499	176,210
74	2,718	1.195	1,000		(523)	172,356	185,225

75	2,800	1,219	1,000	(581)	177,844	194,298
76	2,,884	1,243	1,000	(640)	182,973	203,408
77	2,970	1,268	1,000	(702)	187,685	212,531
76	2,884	1,294	1,000	(766)	191,920	221,642
78	3,059	1,319	1,000	(832)	195,611	230,711
Etc.						

Working During Retirement

When you retire with a hefty balance in your IRA portfolio, you probably won't have to work anymore. Depending upon when you retire, however, you may still want to keep busy. Unless you're a pro or champion amateur, there are only so many golf and/or tennis games you can fit into a week. Table 10-4 lists the advantages and disadvantages of working during retirement.

Table 10-4: Working during Retirement

Advantages	Disadvantages
When you retire early and work (even part-time), you can continue contributing to your IRAs, even if you are making periodic withdrawals from them.	Employers are increasingly offering "contract" employment arrangements, which include few, if any, employee benefits.
Extra income can help pay some of those bills — medical, travel, and hobbies, for example — likely to increase as you get older.	Too much post retirement employment income can adversely affect Social Security benefits. (See Chapter 2 for details.)
	The more you earn, the higher your tax bracket is.

CLIFFSNOTES REVIEW

Use this CliffsNotes Review to practice what you've learned in this book and to build your confidence in doing the job right the first time. After you work through the review questions and the problem-solving exercises, you're well on your way to achieving your goal of investing in IRAs.

Q&A

1. What are the benefits of an IRA? (*Circle all that apply.*)

   a. Savings for long-term goals like retirement, a first home, or college education

   b. Tax-free growth of deposits

   c. Choices of deductible and non-deductible contributions (deposits)

   d. Opportunity for tax-free withdrawals, depending upon type of IRA

2. Most working Americans are participating in some sort of qualified retirement plan. Which of the following can an individual have? (*Circle all that apply.*)

   a. Pension, profit-sharing, or stock bonus plan offered by an employer

   b. An annuity plan or a tax-sheltered annuity contract

   c. IRA, individual retirement (savings) account, or IRA, individual retirement annuity

   d. All of the above

3. Sometimes called an ordinary or regular IRA, the Traditional IRA enables you to (*circle all that apply*):

   a. Deduct some or all of your contributions to it from taxable income

   b. Not pay taxes on your IRA, including earnings and gains, until they are withdrawn (distributed) from the account

   c. Make contributions to your IRA until the age of 70½

   d. Make withdrawals only after you retire

4. An IRA must be opened with a trustee or custodian institution, usually:

   a. Bank, savings association, or credit union

   b. Registered securities dealer

   c. Licensed life insurance company

   d. Any of the above

5. The most that you can contribute for any year to your Traditional IRA is (*circle the correct amounts*):

   a. $4,000 for a single head of household

   b. $2,000 or your income for the year (if less than $2,000)

   c. $4,000 per year for married joint filers

6. True or False: If you have more than one IRA, the limits apply to the total contributions to all Traditional IRAs for the year.

7. True or False: You do not have to contribute to your Traditional IRA every tax year, even if you can.

8. True or False: Your IRA's assets stop growing when you miss or skip contributions.

9. At 59½, you can begin making withdrawals from any Traditional
IRA; at what age *must* you begin making withdrawals?

a. 65 1/2

b. 70½

c. Whenever you officially retire

10. Name four differences between the Roth IRA and the Traditional IRA:

a. _____

b. _____

c. _____

d. _____

11. An Education IRA is (*circle all that apply*)

a. An IRA that can be used to save for college and/or retirement

b. Not really an IRA, but a trust fund to save tax-free funds for higher education until the beneficiary becomes 18 years old

c. An education savings account into which you can deposit up to $2,000 annually for as long as you wish

Answers: 1. a, b, c, and d 2. d.. 3. a, b, and c. 4. d. 5. b or c. 6. T. 7. T. 8. F. 9. b. 10. Roth IRA contributions are not tax deductible, Roth IRA earnings and growth are tax free, Roth IRA withdrawals are generally tax free, Roth IRA withdrawals can be made five years after setting up the account for first home, college education, disability or after 59½ but don't have to be made during the owner's lifetime. 11. B

Scenarios

1. You have a Traditional IRA in which you have accumulated a balance of $21,000 after making regular contributions for seven years. You are 36 years old, married, earn a decent salary, and plan to continue IRA contributions as part of your retirement savings plan. Your family is growing, and your first child is on the way. Your spouse is an independent consultant. What are some options you and your spouse have about funding your future child's education?

2. When Mrs. Jones dies in 1999, her Roth IRA contains regular contributions of $4,000, a conversion contribution of $10,000 that she made in 1998, and earnings of $2,000. No distributions had been made from her IRA. She did not elect to pay the tax on the entire conversion contribution in 1998. Each of her four children had been named as equal beneficiaries. How would you allocate the assets of Mrs. Jones' Roth IRA?

Answers: (1) Your Traditional IRA can be a ready source for higher education funds when the child begins college. However, even though you can tap this source penalty-free, it would reduce your retirement nest egg, and you would have to pay taxes when you withdrew funds. Another option would be to start an Education IRA for the child upon its birth, contributing $500 a year until he or she reaches 18, thus having a tax free fund for the child's college education until his or her 30th birthday. (2) Each child receives an immediate distribution of one-fourth of each type of contribution — regular and conversion — and one-fourth of the earnings: $1,000 from regular contributions + $2,500 from conversion + $500 from earnings = $4,000 to each child. Because the distributions are made before the end of the 5-year period, each child includes $500 in taxable income for 1999.

Consider This

■ Did you know if you are self-employed, you can set up a SIM-PLE IRA for yourself with salary reduction payments of up to $6,000 annually?

■ Did you know you can roll over assets from an employer's retirement plan to a Traditional IRA tax free?

Practice Projects

1. Set up a retirement budget for yourself (and spouse, if you are married). See Chapter 2 for more information.

2. You and your spouse have decided to open a Roth IRA and Education IRAs for two minor children in your family. Determine how much you can contribute to each account. See Chapter 4 for more information.

3. You have just inherited a Traditional IRA and a Roth IRA from your deceased spouse. Decide what you will do with each account. See Chapter 8 for more information.

CLIFFSNOTES RESOURCE CENTER

The learning doesn't need to stop here. CliffsNotes Resource Center shows you the best of the best — links to the best information in print and online about IRAs. And don't think that this is all we've prepared for you. We've put all kinds of pertinent information at www.cliffsnotes.com. Look for these terrific resources at your favorite bookstore or local library and on the Internet. When online, make your first stop www.cliffsnotes.com where you'll find more useful information about IRAs and retirement planning.

Books

This CliffNotes book is one of many great books about investing for your retirement published by IDG Books Worldwide, Inc. So if you want some great next-step books, check out these other publications:

- **Investing For Dummies,** by Eric Tyson. For a more in-depth discussion of the full range of investment possibilities open to you — from real estate to venture capital — this book is a great source of information. IDG Books Worldwide, Inc., $19.99.

- **Personal Finance For Dummies,** by Eric Tyson. With the help of this book, you can learn to manage your money efficiently, reduce your debts, and save more of your income. IDG Books Worldwide, Inc., $19.99.

- **Life and Death Planning for Retirement Benefits, 1998 Supplement,** by Natalie B. Choate. This is an essential handbook for estate planners. Ataxplan Publications, $39.95.

- **Roth IRA Book: An Investor's Guide,** by Gobind Daryanani. This book clearly presents comparisons of the different kinds of IRAs. Great for those who are considering including the Roth IRA in their retirement plans. Pricewaterhouse Coopers, $34.95.

- **IRA Investing Made Easy: A Beginners Guide to Successful IRA Strategies,** by Anna Marie Hutchison. This book is aimed primarily at the average person who wants to take charge of his or her own investments for retirement. Globe Pequot, $12.95.

- **Kiplinger's Practical Guide to Your Money,** by Ted Miller. Comprehensive work about how to handle your money, your property, your insurance, your investments, your retirement, and estate planning. Kiplinger Books, $29.95.

- **How to Retire Rich: Time-Tested Strategies to Beat the Market and Retire in Style**, by James P. O'Shaughnessy. This book offers detailed presentations of how to manage investments in stocks, bonds, and mutual funds, plus pitfalls to avoid. Broadway Books, $25.00.

It's easy to find books published by IDG Books Worldwide, Inc. And other publishers. You'll find them in your favorite bookstores (on the Internet and at a store near you). We also have three Web sites that you can use to read about all the books we publish:

- www.cliffsnotes.com

- www.dummies.com

- www.idgbooks.com

Internet

Check out these Web sites for more information about IRAs, retirement planning, and more:

- **Internal Revenue Service,** www.irs.gov — IRS publications and forms, questions and answers about IRAs available here.

- **DQI Inc.-Roth IRA Service Provider,** www.dqi-roth.com — Roth IRA service provider, using high-end software.

- **Roth Ira Web Site Home Page,** www.rothira.com — Wide range of IRA topics: news, calculators, links to articles in newspapers and magazines, special feature articles.

- **Management Account Services, Inc.,** www.fee-only-advisor.com — Online book "Investment Strategies For the 21st Century," by Frank Armstrong, Miami, FL, 1999.

- **Fairmark Press: Tax Guide for Investors,** www.fairmark.com — Explains rules for Roth IRAs.

- **Financial Engines, Inc.,** www.financialengines.com — Retirement planning calculator that tests millions of possible economic and investment outcomes.

- **Fidelity Investment,** www.fidelity.com — Roth IRA conversion calculator and articles. Free software.

- **Northwestern Mutual Life,** www.northwesternmutual.com — Roth IRA calculator and a "longevity game" to determine your life expectancy.

- **Strong on-line,** www.strongfunds.com — Compares future outcomes for Roth IRA compared to Traditional IRA. Free software

■ **Access Vanguard(tm),** www.vanguard.com — Variety of retirement savings resources. Free software.

Next time you're on the Internet, don't forget to drop by www.cliffsnotes.com. We created an online Resource Center that you an use today, tomorrow, and beyond.

Other Resources

Following are some agencies that can help you find information about IRAs, eligibility, and so on:

■ **Internal Revenue Service (Treasury Dept.),** Washington, DC. www.irs.ustreas.gov — Answers to tax questions, fill-in forms, publications, and more.

■ **Social Security Administration,** Baltimore, MD — Maintains earnings and beneficiary records; makes changes in beneficiary records for retirement, survivors and disability insurance. Phone: (800) 772-1213, Fax (410) 965-1344.

■ **Federal Reserve Board, Banking Supervision & Regulatory Division,** Washington, DC. www.bog.frb.fed.us — Hears complaints about practices of financial institutions that are members of the Federal Reserve System. Phone (202) 452-2773; Fax (202-452-2770.

■ **SEC, Securities and Exchange Commission,** Washington, DC. www.sec.gov — Oversees dealers in registered securities. Phone (202) 942-0100; Fax (202) 942-9646.

■ **FDIC, Federal Deposit Insurance Corporation,** Washington, DC. www.fdic.gov — Insures your deposits at member banks, savings and loans, and mutual savings banks up to $100,000 per account. Phone (202) 874-5060; Fax (202) 874-5293.

- **NCUA, National Credit Union Administration,** Alexandria, VA.. www.ncua.gov — Insures your deposits at member credit unions up to $100,000 per account. Phone (703) 518-6300; Fax (703) 518-6319.

- **NASD National Association of Securities Dealers,** Washington, DC. www.nasd.com — Arbitrates disputes between investors and brokerage firms regulated by the SEC. Phone (202) 728-8000; Fax (202728-8075.

- **U.S. General Services Administration Consumer Information Center.** www.pueblo.gsa.gov — Publishes free books, including "1998-99 Consumer Resource Handbook," which includes listings of all public agencies in all 50 states and U.S. possessions. State banking and credit regulatory agencies are among these listings.

Send Us Your Favorite Tips

In your quest for learning, have you ever experienced that sublime moment when you figure out a trick that saves time or trouble? Perhaps you realized you were taking ten steps to accomplish something that could have taken two. Or you found a little-known workaround that gets great results. If you've discovered a useful tip that helped you ask the right questions about IRAs or invest more effectively and you'd like to share it, the CliffsNotes staff would love to hear from you. Go to our Web site at www.cliffsnotes.com and click the Talk to Us button. If we select your tip, we may publish it as part of CliffsNotes Daily, our exciting, free e-mail newsletter. To find out more or to subscribe to a newsletter, go to on the Web.

INDEX

CliffsNotes™

Your shortcut to
success™
for over 40 years

Computers and Software
Confused by computers? Struggling with software? Let
CliffsNotes get you up to speed on the fundamentals —
quickly and easily. Titles include:

Balancing Your Checkbook with Quicken®
Buying Your First PC
Creating a Dynamite PowerPoint® 2000 Presentation
Making Windows® 98 Work for You
Setting up a Windows® 98 Home Network
Upgrading and Repairing Your PC
Using Your First PC
Using Your First iMac™
Writing Your First Computer Program

The Internet
Intrigued by the Internet? Puzzled about life online?
Let *CliffsNotes* show you how to get started with e-mail,
Web surfing, and more. Titles include:

Buying and Selling on eBay®
Creating Web Pages with HTML
Creating Your First Web Page
Exploring the Internet with Yahoo!®
Finding a Job on the Web
Getting on the Internet
Going Online with AOL®
Shopping Online Safely